THE

HISTORY

ATLAS OF

AFRICA

The Macmillan Continental History Atlases

The History Atlas of Africa
The History Atlas of Asia
The History Atlas of Europe
The History Atlas of North America
The History Atlas of South America

THE

HISTORY

ATLAS OF

AFRICA

Samuel Kasule

MACMILLAN • USA

MACMILLAN

A Simon & Schuster Macmillan Company
1633 Broadway
New York, NY 10019-6785

Library of Congress Cataloging-in-Publication Data

Kasule, Samuel, Dr.
      The Macmillan history atlas of Africa / Samuel Kasule.
          p.   cm.
      Includes bibliographical references and index.
      ISBN 0–02–862580–3 (hardcover)
      1. Africa—Historical geography—Maps.   I. Title.   II. Title:
History atlas of Africa.   III. Title: Atlas of Africa
G2446.S1 K3   1998   <G&M>
911'.6—DC21

                                            98–12839
                                                CIP
                                              MAPS

Manufactured in the United States
10 9 8 7 6 5 4 3 2 1

FOREWORD

The shifting patterns of global politics since the collapse of Soviet influence and the liberation of South Africa have radically repositioned the African continent in contemporary world history. *The History Atlas of Africa* offers a timely background study of this widely neglected subject, presenting African history in a way that reflects Africans' own views.

The atlas explores Africa's human history from the evolution of the first hominids, through the pre-historical ages, the ancient empires, the colonial period, and post-independence, to the contemporary era. Recent archaeological discoveries have shown that the history of "the black people" stretches far back into the remote African past, encompassing the development of agriculture and the Iron Age. More recently, the continent has witnessed migrations, conquests, and occupations by Europeans and Arabs, resulting in the rich mixture of contrasting economic, social, artistic, and religious beliefs and practices that it boasts today. Africa to the north of the Sahara is here contrasted with Africa to the south, the Egyptian civilization with those of Benin and Zimbabwe.

The Roman and Byzantine conquests of North Africa were restricted to the coastal strip between Egypt and Mauretania (Morocco), while the spread of Islam from the Middle East, following the decline of the Byzantines, led to the development of great sub-Saharan trading cities. Long before the arrival of the European colonizers, Arabic scholars, geographers and merchants, such as al Bakri, al Fazari, and Ibn Battuta recorded the wealth and splendor of these cities. This atlas includes studies of these often overlooked pre-European cultures.

The spread of Islam and Arabic divided the continent north and south of the Sahara, and these north-south differences were accentuated by the arrival of European colonizers, the transatlantic slave trade, the nineteenth-century spread of Christianity, and the new directions of trade and politics. African and Swahili civilizations were destroyed, while the American and Caribbean connections forged by the slave trade became the cornerstone of the continent's new historical orientation. African religious, agricultural, and artistic traditions have formed the heritage now enjoyed by the descendants of those transported slaves. The atlas includes studies of the African diaspora throughout the Americas, Europe, and Asia.

Contemporary political conflicts are rooted in Africa's past. The effects of European colonial rule, and of the continent's sometimes arbitrary partition between 1880 and 1914, are here examined. Because the new boundaries often disregarded the politics of the pre-colonial "states," the consequences of partition have continued to haunt post-independence Africa in the form of secessionist conflicts such as those in Uganda, Rwanda, Congo, and Nigeria. In this atlas, the roots of such conflicts in the colonial history of subjugation, collaboration, and resistance are explored.

Post-independence Africa has witnessed the rise and fall of several despots, as well as a range of experiments in multi-party democracy and one-party systems rooted in traditional African political structures. With the disintegration of the Eastern bloc and the multinational visit to Africa in March 1998 by U.S. president Bill Clinton, the continent is assuming a new globally strategic role (one that this book, I hope, will prove an aid to understanding).

Dr. Samuel Kasule

CONTENTS

THE

HISTORY

ATLAS OF

AFRICA

PART I: EARLY HUMANS

Homo habilis evolved in Africa some three to two and-a-half million years ago, co-existent with Australopithicus africanus *and* Australopithecus robustus. *However, it was* Homo habilis *who probably developed the use of tools and provided the line of development from which sprang more modern forms of the human species.*

Africa provides the earliest known evidence of human existence. Between three and a half and four million years ago, small-brained hominids lived in the African grasslands, using stone choppers to kill prey. About one million years ago they developed better tools, such as hand axes with two cutting edges, and between fifty and sixty thousand years ago, they began using fire to cook food and learned how to fashion wood.

The Stone Age may be divided into three periods. During the Early Stone Age, primitive man used hand axes, remains of which have been found in eastern Africa. In the Middle Stone Age, between 50,000 and 15,000 BC, with new tool-making skills, he spread throughout the continent. In the Late Stone Age, by around 8000 BC, he had evolved some way from the Neanderthal, Rhodesian, Mousterian, or Sangoan men of the Stone Age cultures and had come to resemble present-day *Homo sapiens*.

Information about Late Stone Age man's way of life and beliefs may be gleaned from rock paintings and engravings found from the Sahara in the north to South Africa. In eastern, central, and southern Africa, many rock shelters and caves were settled, especially near water supplies, and at some sites, such as Gambles Cave in Kenya, archaeologists have found burial remains that provide evidence of religious practices. Tanzania has the largest number of examples of animal and human depictions, mostly concentrated in the Kondoa region and around Lake Eyasi.

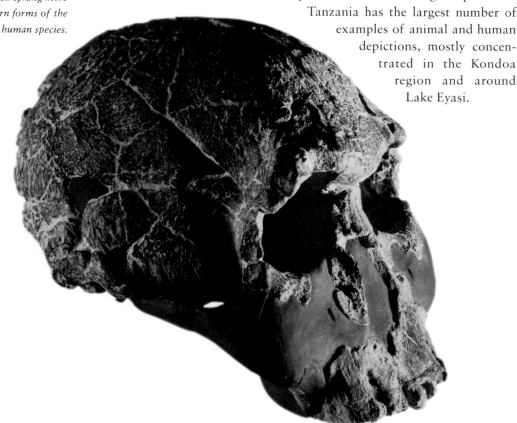

The dividing features of humans and apes are the size and development of the brain, jaw, and upright posture. This divide is believed to have occurred some five to seven million years ago.

The first homonids were australopithecines ("southern apes"). The oldest, Australopithecus ramidus, *is known from a few bone fragments; however,* Austrolopithecus aferensis *is better understood from the skeleton of a female, "Lucy," who stood about three feet (one meter) tall. A larger creature,* Australopithecus africanus, *appeared some two million years ago; after that, evolution forks, one branch to a dead end, the other leading to* Homo habilis *("the skillful man") and* Homo erectus, *and eventually to* Homo sapiens sapiens, *who via their many local adaptations have become masters of the planet.*

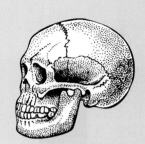

HOMO SAPIENS

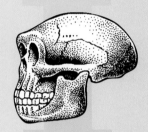

HOMO ERECTUS

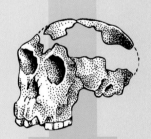

HOMO HABILIS

AUSTRALOPITHECUS ROBUSTUS

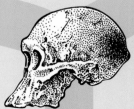

AUSTRALOPITHECUS AFRICANUS

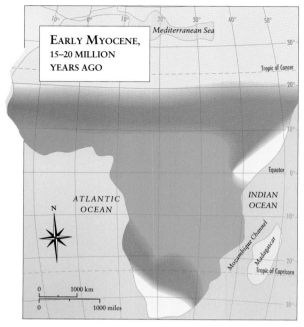

VEGETATION

☐ desert	☐ moist woodland
☐ macchia	☐ lowland forest
☐ dry woodland and bushland	☐ montane forest

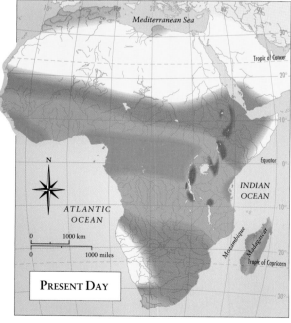

Classification of the early human populations is aided by language families and by settlement sites, which relate to the fertility of the surrounding land and to the tools made by and available to their inhabitants.

The distinctive family groupings that inhabited Africa by the time of the Iron Age were the Negroes, Pygmies, San, Nilo-Saharans, and the Hamito-Semitics and Cushites (Caucasoids) who had migrated from Asia.

Large-scale population movements occurred on the continent, and perhaps by natural selection two groups evolved south of the Sahara: the light-skinned Khoisan, who settled in areas of southern Africa; and the dark-skinned Negroes adapted to the savannahs and woodlands, who originated in the west and and who now populate central and southern Africa.

Nilo-Saharans lived around and along the Nile, while the BaMbuti (Pygmies) originated in the Ituri Forest of the Congo Basin. The Khoi-san or Capoid (Bushmen or Hottentots) are now found mainly in the Kalahari desert, but their characteristics are shared by most people in southern Africa, and a subgroup of them still exists in central Tanzania.

Hamito-Semitics, including Berbers and Cushites, combine migrants from the Middle East sharing linguistic styles.

Between 8000 and 2000 BC, climatic and cultural changes forced new methods of tool-making in what is referred to as the Neolithic Revolution. During this period, across Africa, people started making more sophisticated artifacts, including woven baskets, pottery, and constructed shelters.

Primitive farming—the taming of animals and planting of seeds—led to the development of more permanent settlements with secure food supplies capable of sustaining larger communities. Stone Age people colonized forest, hill, and savannah, followed by the masters of metal: first copper, then bronze, and later iron. African civilization had begun.

Two great geophysical extremes affecting African development are, to the north, the Sahara desert, criss-crossed by trade routes linked by widely spread oases (above); and, in west and central Africa, the dense rainforest, penetrated by river links and trackways (below).

THE ORIGINS OF HUMANKIND

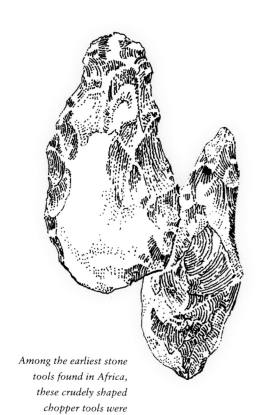

Among the earliest stone tools found in Africa, these crudely shaped chopper tools were found in East Africa and date from about 200,000 years ago.

Africa saw the genesis of humanity. The fossil remains discovered in its east, south, and north hold the key to our origins. Although this a subject of much uncertainty and debate, it appears that several million years ago, while the North American and European continents were frozen, Africa became steadily drier. The desertification of the Sahara deprived the wildlife of flourishing grasslands and formed a northern east-west barrier, while forest divided central Africa from the west. Other areas like the east and south were open grasslands, and the Kalahari in the southwest and most areas of the northeast were deserts. Some of the savannah's primate inhabitants evolved a new bipedal (two-legged) method of walking, and with freed hands, these early hominid Australopithecines ("southern apes") began to hunt.

Remains of Australopithecines found only in Africa over four million years old have been found in the south at Taung in the Transvaal and in the east at the Olduvai Gorge, the Omo Valley, and Koobi Fora in Tanzania and Kenya. These, and nearby sites that have also yielded remains of our more recent ancestors *Homo habilis*, generally regarded as the first humans.

Later, 1.8 million years ago, *Homo erectus*, a more advanced human, appeared on the archaeological record. Equipped with a larger brain and an easier walking posture, it was *Homo erectus* who probably mastered the use of fire, and made more sophisticated hand axe tools. With this extra knowledge *Homo erectus* left Africa and colonized Eurasia, creating a larger area for human development. It seems likely that our successful distant forbear *Homo habilis*, "the skillful man," and the first toolmaker, may for some while have been contemporary with other Australopithecines.

Besides being able to fashion hand axes and choppers, *Homo erectus*, whose remains have also been found in northern Africa, Java, and China, was probably the hominid who first developed language skills.

Around 400,000 years ago, *Homo sapiens* appeared and had evolved into what we would recognize as modern humans. Perhaps the most well-known sites associated with *Homo sapiens* again are from the opposite ends of the continent, Omo Valley in Ethiopia and Border Cave in South Africa, dating from 100,000 years ago.

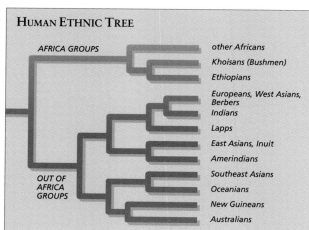

HUMAN ETHNIC TREE

AFRICA GROUPS

- other Africans
- Khoisans (Bushmen)
- Ethiopians
- Europeans, West Asians, Berbers
- Indians
- Lapps
- East Asians, Inuit
- Amerindians
- Southeast Asians
- Oceanians
- New Guineans
- Australians

OUT OF AFRICA GROUPS

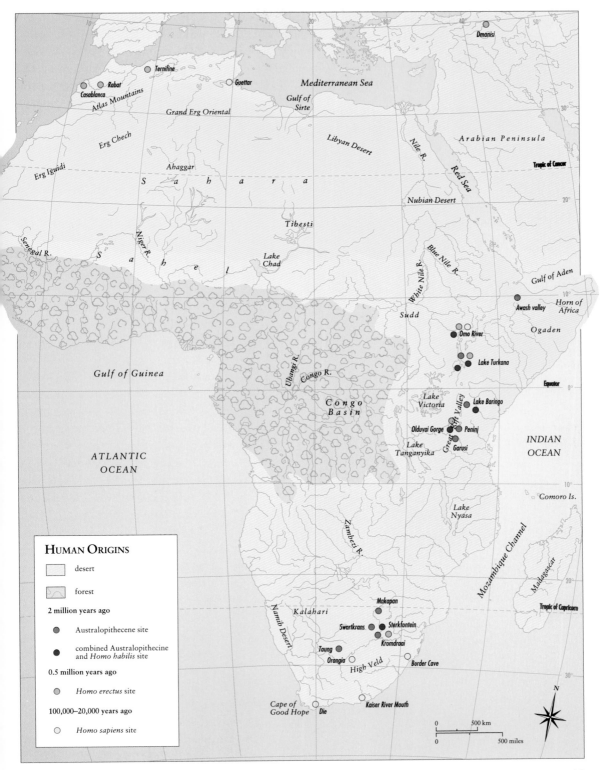

HUMAN ORIGINS

desert

forest

2 million years ago

● Australopithecene site

● combined Australopithecine
and *Homo habilis* site

0.5 million years ago

● *Homo erectus* site

100,000–20,000 years ago

○ *Homo sapiens* site

Mediterranean Sea

Ternifine
Rabat
Casablanca
Atlas Mountains
Guettar
Gulf of Sirte
Grand Erg Oriental
Erg Chech
Erg Iguidi
Ahaggar
S a h a r a
Libyan Desert
Nile R.
Red Sea
Arabian Peninsula
Tropic of Cancer
Nubian Desert
Dmanisi

Senegal R.
Niger R.
S a h e l
Lake Chad
Tibesti

White Nile R.
Blue Nile R.
Gulf of Aden
Awash valley
Horn of Africa
Ogaden
Sudd

Gulf of Guinea
Ubangi R.
Congo R.
Congo Basin
Omo River
Lake Turkana
Equator

Lake Victoria
Great Rift Valley
Lake Baringo
Olduvai Gorge
Peninj
Garusi
Lake Tanganyika

ATLANTIC OCEAN

INDIAN OCEAN

Comoro Is.
Lake Nyasa

Zambezi R.
Mozambique Channel
Madagascar

Namib Desert
Kalahari
Makapan
Swartkrans
Sterkfontein
Kromdraai
Taung
Orangia
High Veld
Border Cave
Tropic of Capricorn

Cape of Good Hope
Die
Kaiser River Mouth

N

0   500 km
0   500 miles

HUMAN DIVERSITY

The Sahel and the grasslands of East Africa, a zone through which Nilo Saharans and Cushite peoples extended their range.

Skeletal remains of Middle Stone Age inhabitants of Africa have been found at early settlement sites, like the "Rhodesian Man" discovered at Kabwe ("Broken Hill") in what is now Zambia in 1921. His features are similar to those of the Neanderthal men discovered in Europe and also found at sites in North Africa, displaying full-sized braincases and heavy, massive bones. Similar fossils have been found at Olduvai Gorge and Saldanha Bay in South Africa.

The map shows the sites where remains of Neanderthal man, Rhodesian man, and modern man have been found.

The process of classification is linguistically influenced, and settlement patterns are also related to the fertility of the land and tools available to their inhabitants. Several different families of Africans lived on the continent by the time of the Iron Age, during which the "tall" hunters were superseded by the "short" hunters, BaMbuti, and Khoisan (Bushmen).

Anthropologists recognize the following distinctive African population groupings: Negroes, BaMbuti (Pygmies), San, Nilo-Saharans, and Hamito-Semitics (Berbers and Cushites).

Negroes originated in West Africa, and adapted to the savannah and woodlands north of the equatorial forests. They are big, black-skinned, broad-nosed, and curly-haired, and are the descendents of Late Stone Age man in eastern and western Africa.

BaMbuti (Pygmies) originated in the Congo (Zaire), are small, short, of light or dark complexion, and are broad-nosed and sparse-haired.

Nilo-Saharans have similar features to the Negroes' but are thinner and taller, and live around and along the Nile River.

San are bigger, yellow, brown, or black, and have close-cropped hair and large buttocks. They are found mainly in the Kalahari desert, but their characteristics are shared by most people in southern Africa. This group also includes the Khoisan or Capoid (Bushmen and Hottentots).

Hamito-Semitics, migrants from the Middle East who share linguistic styles, include the Berbers and the Cushites. They are tall, long-headed, and light-skinned.

Map labels:

BERBERS
HAMITO-SEMITIC
Mediterranean Sea
EGYPTIANS
SEMITES GROUP
Tropic of Cancer
Sahara Desert
NILO-SAHARANS
NEGROES
CUSHITES
N
ATLANTIC OCEAN
PYGMIES
Equator
INDIAN OCEAN
0   1000 km
0   1000 miles
Mozambique Channel
Madagascar
SAN
Kalahari Desert
Tropic of Capricorn

POPULATION MOVEMENTS
TO c. 2000 BC

→ major population group migration

- - - Sahel 'corridor'

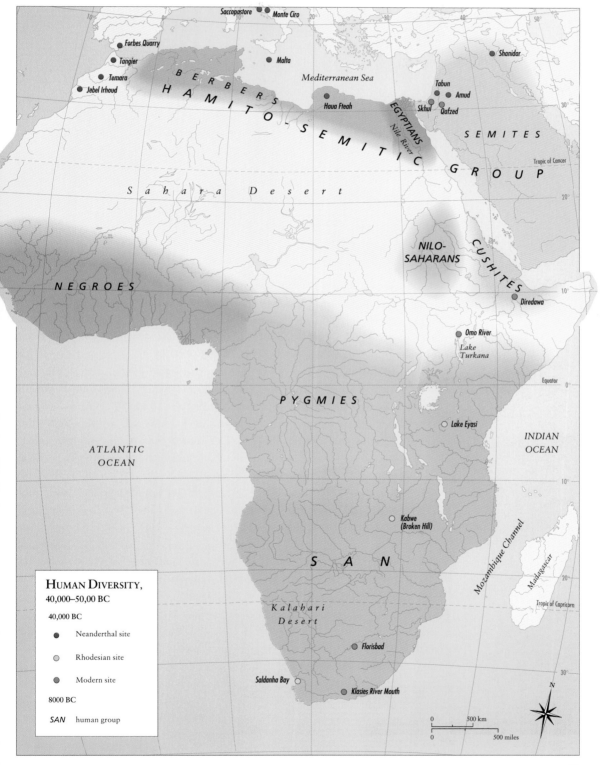

Saccopastore
Monte Ciro
Forbes Quarry
Tangier
Temara
Jebel Irhoud
Malta
Shanidar

BERBERS
HAMITO-SEMITIC

Mediterranean Sea

Tabun
Amud
Skhul
Qafzed

Haua Fteah

EGYPTIANS

Nile River

SEMITES

GROUP

Tropic of Cancer

Sahara Desert

NILO-
SAHARANS

CUSHITES

NEGROES

Diredawa

Omo River

Lake
Turkana

Equator

PYGMIES

Lake Eyasi

INDIAN
OCEAN

ATLANTIC
OCEAN

Kabwe
(Broken Hill)

SAN

Mozambique Channel

Madagascar

Tropic of Capricorn

Kalahari
Desert

Florisbad

Saldanha Bay

Klasies River Mouth

HUMAN DIVERSITY,
40,000–50,00 BC

40,000 BC

- ●   Neanderthal site
- ○   Rhodesian site
- ●   Modern site

8000 BC

SAN   human group

0   500 km

0   500 miles

N

DEVELOPMENT OF AGRICULTURE

Farmed for almost 4,000 years, these fields are in the Ethiopian highlands.

People in Africa have obtained food by many different methods. In early times they gathered and hunted, but by the end of the Middle Stone Age they had discovered agriculture. While agricultural skills began in the area that is now Iran, Iraq, and Syria, the domestication of some food plants started in Africa, especially along the Nile Valley, the first site, as early as 6000 BC, of planted crops such as sorghum, millet, and yams. The farming activity along the Nile River may have continued alongside hunting, gathering, and fishing, for established agricultural communities did not appear there until about 5000 BC, nor did animal husbandry, which originated in the Ethiopian highlands, until about 4000 BC.

The rearing of goats, sheep, and cattle then probably spread from the northeast to other parts of Africa south of the Sahara that were free from tsetse flies. There were varieties of cattle in the west and northeast as far back as the Late Stone Age, and other varieties like Zebu and Sanga were introduced in eastern and central Africa during the Early Iron Age as the human population expanded. Fishing became a highly specialized activity with the development of "barbed bone points," which have been found at sites on Lakes Katwe and Victoria. Evidence of man's primitive agricultural way of life is also found in rock paintings such as those of the Kondoa district of Tanzania.

In western Africa, the movement to food production was strengthened by the adoption of indigenous yams, oil-palm, potato, and shea butter trees. These, combined with crops like corn and cassava, later imported from the New World, led to the establishment of fixed settlements in specific areas.

Africa is also the second-generation center for crops like bananas, sugar cane, and citrus fruits. The banana, a native of southeast Asia, was probably introduced by Indonesian sailors after AD 300 and remains popular in Uganda and other parts of eastern and central Africa. Around AD 700, Asian rice was introduced by Arab sailors, while north of the Sahara, barley and wheat were grown.

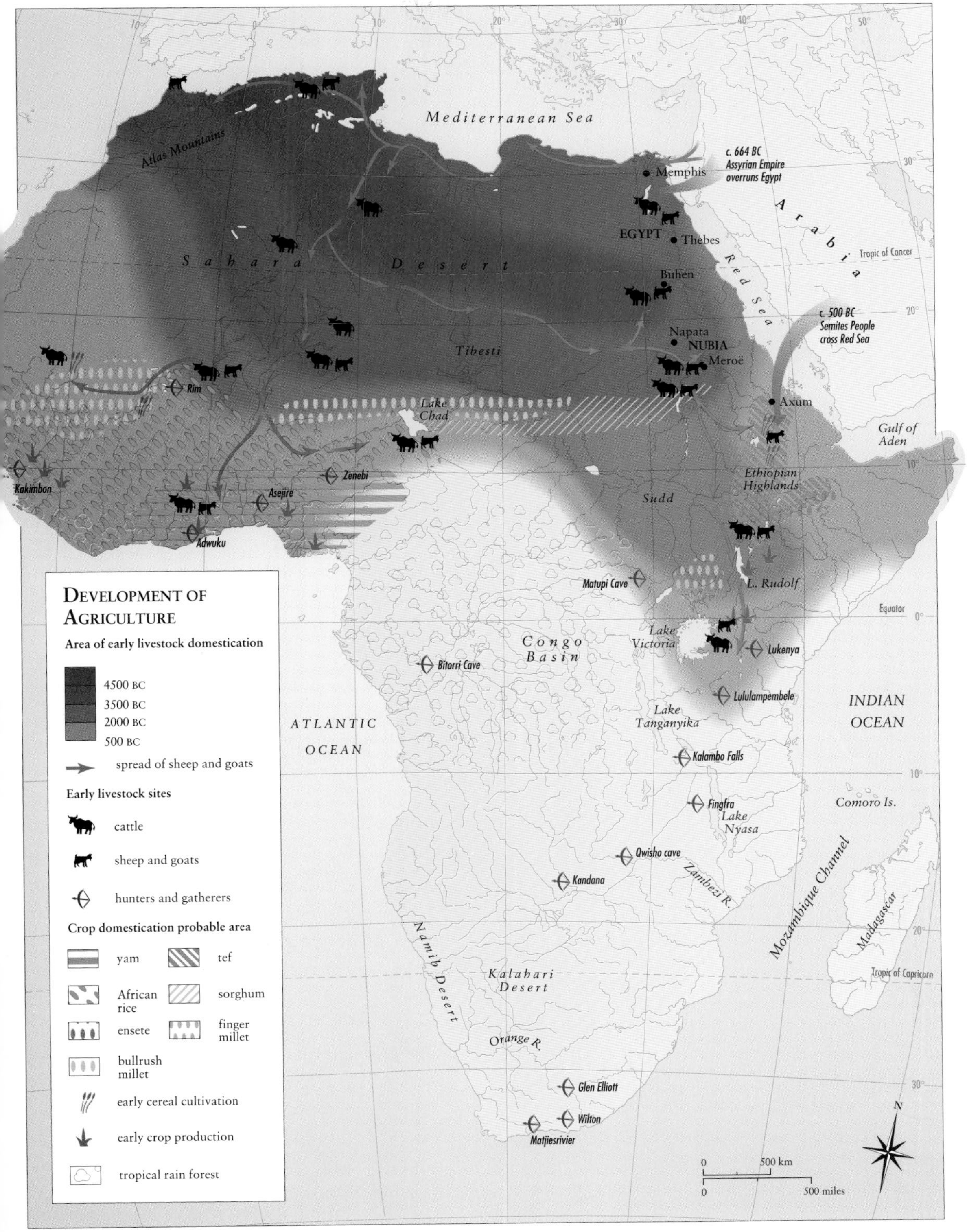
Mediterranean Sea
Atlas Mountains
Sahara Desert
Tibesti
Memphis
c. 664 BC Assyrian Empire overruns Egypt
EGYPT
Thebes
Arabia
Red Sea
Tropic of Cancer
Buhen
Napata
NUBIA
Meroë
c. 500 BC Semites People cross Red Sea
Axum
Gulf of Aden
Ethiopian Highlands
Sudd
Lake Chad
Rim
Kakimbon
Zenebi
Asejire
Adwuku
Matupi Cave
L. Rudolf
Equator
Lake Victoria
Lukenya
Congo Basin
Bitorri Cave
Lululampembele
Lake Tanganyika
INDIAN OCEAN
ATLANTIC OCEAN
Kalambo Falls
Fingira
Lake Nyasa
Comoro Is.
Qwisho cave
Zambezi R.
Kandana
Mozambique Channel
Madagascar
Namib Desert
Kalahari Desert
Tropic of Capricorn
Orange R.
Glen Elliott
Wilton
Matjiesrivier
0 500 km
0 500 miles
N
Development of Agriculture
Area of early livestock domestication
4500 BC
3500 BC
2000 BC
500 BC
spread of sheep and goats
Early livestock sites
cattle
sheep and goats
hunters and gatherers
Crop domestication probable area
yam
tef
African rice
sorghum
ensete
finger millet
bullrush millet
early cereal cultivation
early crop production
tropical rain forest

THE IRON AGE

The Iron Age, a period of almost 2,000 years, witnessed migration, agricultural expansion and specialization, and population increase. In the Late Stone Age, aided by the spread of metalworking, there were new developments in crop cultivation and pastoralism. The earliest metal to be worked was copper, which was smelted and mixed with tin to produce bronze. While the earliest copper-working site is in the Sinai, copper and bronze were widely used in Egypt and along the Mediterranean coast, and there is evidence of early copper-working in western Africa, central Niger, and at Akjoujt in Mauritania. Three specific trade routes across the Sahara from central Niger are evidenced by rock engravings around copper-making regions stretching into northern Morocco. At around 900 BC Berbers from the north began to spread iron-smelting skills through the region from Carthage.

Evidence of old channeled or dimple-cased pottery has been used to show that the Iron Age in Africa probably began in its eastern, central, and western regions, leading to increased population and migration. Around AD 300, Iron Age people had settled at Great Zimbabwe in southern Africa and later, in the copper-rich area of Katanga in the Congo. Settlements like these were initiated by early farmers and herdsmen, and by smelters of iron and workers with clay. The discovery of old pottery helps to locate Iron Age settlements and to identify their inhabitants, and this evidence suggests that by AD 900 these settlements had evolved into social groups with recognized leaders.

The spread of distinct, settled societies generated different linguistic groups, as the Iron Age witnessed the expansion of the Zande and Bantu from the west. From the Cameroon mountains, the Bantu spread across equatorial Africa to the Congo basin and as far as the White Nile. With the advantage of metal tools and weapons, they settled around the East African rift valley and Lake Victoria, displacing the BaMbuti and the Khoisan. The former withdrew deep into the Ituri Forest, while the latter moved south.

A reconstruction of the Axumite palace at Enda Mika'el Axum. This building combines the best of both worlds, a lavishly decorated home together with secure fortifications.

20

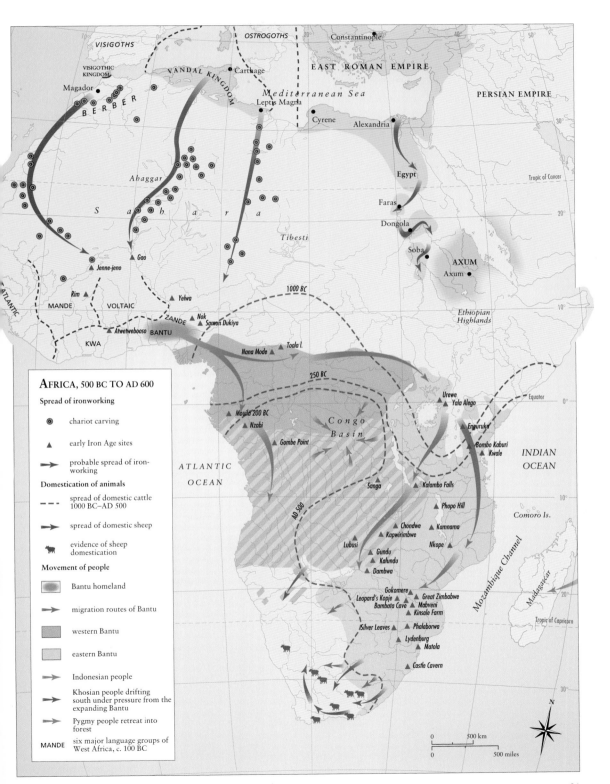

VISIGOTHS

OSTROGOTHS

Constantinople

VISIGOTHIC
KINGDOM

VANDAL KINGDOM

Carthage

EAST ROMAN EMPIRE

Magador

B E R B E R

Leptis Magna

Mediterranean Sea

PERSIAN EMPIRE

Cyrene

Alexandria

Ahaggar

Egypt

Tropic of Cancer

S a h a r a

Faras

Dongola

Tibesti

Soba

AXUM

Axum

Gao

Jenne-jeno

*Ethiopian
Highlands*

Rim

MANDE   VOLTAIC

1000 BC

Yelwa

ZANDE

Nok

Samon Dukiya

Afwetwebooso   BANTU

KWA

Nana Mode

Toala I.

250 BC

Mouila 200 BC

Nzabi

*C o n g o
B a s i n*

Urewe
Yala Alego

Equator

Engaruka

Gombe Point

ATLANTIC

OCEAN

Bombo Kaburi
Kwale

INDIAN

OCEAN

Sanga

Kalambo Falls

AD 500

Phopo Hill

Comoro Is.

Chondwe
Kapwirimbwe

Kamnama

Lubusi

Nkope

Gundu
Kalundu

Dambwa

*M
o
z
a
m
b
i
q
u
e

C
h
a
n
n
e
l*

Gokomere

Leopard's Kopje
Bambata Cave

Great Zimbabwe

Mabveni

*M
a
d
a
g
a
s
c
a
r*

Kinsale Farm

Silver Leaves

Phalaborwa

Tropic of Capricorn

Lydenburg
Matola

Castle Cavern

N

AFRICA, 500 BC TO AD 600

Spread of ironworking

⊙   chariot carving

▲   early Iron Age sites

→   probable spread of iron-
    working

Domestication of animals

- - -   spread of domestic cattle
        1000 BC–AD 500

→   spread of domestic sheep

🐂   evidence of sheep
    domestication

Movement of people

▦   Bantu homeland

→   migration routes of Bantu

▨   western Bantu

▨   eastern Bantu

→   Indonesian people

→   Khosian people drifting
    south under pressure from the
    expanding Bantu

→   Pygmy people retreat into
    forest

MANDE   six major language groups of
        West Africa, c. 100 BC

0   500 km

0   500 miles

AFRICAN LANGUAGES

Africa's linguistic landscape is complex. There are estimated to be about 1,500 languages altogether, ranging from those spoken by millions of people as a first or second language, including Arabic, Swahili, Fula, and Hausa, to those languages spoken by merely a handful.

Linguists group together languages that are mutually intelligible. For example, Luganda, Runyankole, and Lusoga in Uganda have easily recognizable similarities, as do Zulu and Xhosa. The map is based on the classification of J. H. Greenberg, who identified four main African language families: Niger-Congo, originally spoken to the west of Lake Chad; the Chari-Nile (Nilo-Saharan) negroid languages; Afro-Asiatic, spoken by the Caucasoid peoples of the north and northeast; and Khoisan, the click languages of the San.

Along the West African coast the Wolo and Fulani groupings predominate, while the languages of the Kwa family are spoken in southern Nigeria (Yoruba and Ibo), and by the Mande people of the Upper Volta and Niger regions (Malinke, Soninke, and Bambara).

In East Africa there are three unrelated language families: Bantu, Nilotic, and Cushitic. The Bantu languages of the Niger-Congo family are spoken mostly in Congo and in eastern, central, and southern Africa, while others of the family are spoken only in western Africa. Their origin is an area in eastern Nigeria and Cameroon, and they all share certain features, such as the root *ntu,* denoting humanness, and the prefix *ba,* denoting plurality. As the Bantu spread, their languages were adopted by the BaMbuti and other inhabitants of the lands they occupied.

The Chari-Nile family includes Moru-Madi of central and southern Sudan, northeastern Congo, and the Central African Republic.

The Nilotic family spreads throughout East Africa, dividing into three branches: Highland (Kalenjin in western Kenya, Dadog and Dorobo in Tanzania); Plains (Maasai in Kenya and Tanzania, Itunga, Karamajong-Teso, Bari and Kakwaand); and River-Lake (Dinka and Nuer in the Sudan, Lwo in Uganda and Kenya).

Greenberg divided the Afro-Asiatic group into five subfamilies: Semitic (including Arabic); Ancient Egyptian; Berber; Chadic (including Hausa); and Cushitic, which is found in southwestern Asia as well as in northern and northeastern Africa (Ethiopia and Somalia).

In the south, the Khoisan, the Sotho, and the Southern Nguni, who inhabit the Kalahari desert and adjacent areas, have preserved their unique click languages made famous to Westerners in the 1950s by African jazz singer Miriam Makeba.

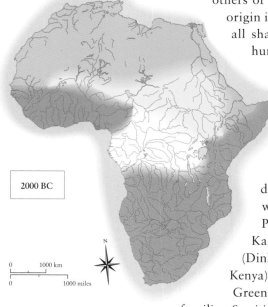

2000 BC

0   1000 km

0   1000 miles

N

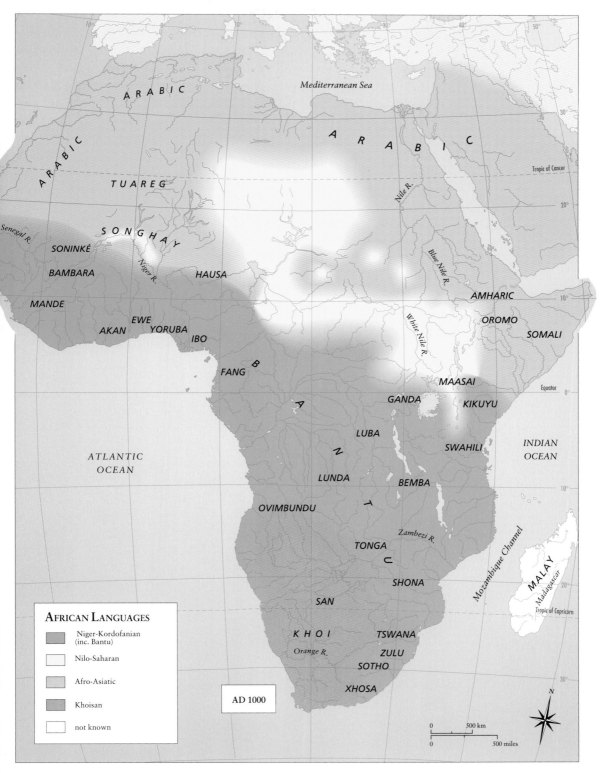

ARABIC

ARABIC

Mediterranean Sea

A R A B I C

Tropic of Cancer

TUAREG

Nile R.

SONGHAY

Senegal R.

SONINKÉ

Blue Nile R.

BAMBARA

Niger R.

HAUSA

AMHARIC

MANDE

OROMO

EWE

SOMALI

AKAN

YORUBA

IBO

B

White Nile R.

FANG

A

MAASAI

GANDA

KIKUYU

ATLANTIC
OCEAN

N

LUBA

SWAHILI

INDIAN
OCEAN

LUNDA

BEMBA

T

OVIMBUNDU

TONGA

C

Zambezi R.

Equator

SHONA

SAN

MALAY

KHOI

TSWANA

Orange R.

ZULU

SOTHO

XHOSA

Tropic of Capricorn

Mozambique Channel

Madagascar

AFRICAN LANGUAGES

- Niger-Kordofanian (inc. Bantu)
- Nilo-Saharan
- Afro-Asiatic
- Khoisan
- not known

AD 1000

0   500 km

0   500 miles

N

PART II: KINGDOMS AND EMPIRES

The neolithic revolution entered Africa through Egypt, whose inhabitants' agricultural skills, and mastery of the Nile River's seasonal flooding, were unmatched by any other community. Their settled way of life led to an increased population and the creation of a unique civilization with a centralized government and a complex administrative system. The Old Kingdom (3110–2258 BC) saw Upper and Lower Egypt for the first time united under a single crown; during the Middle Kingdom (2000–1786 BC) Egypt became increasingly dominated by foreign powers, culminating in invasion by the Hyksos from western Asia; under the New Kingdom (1567–1085 BC) the Egyptians completely occupied Nubia, and later Palestine and Syria. When the New Kingdom disintegrated, King Kashata of Nubia led the first Cushite (Nubian) military expedition against Egypt in 750 BC, and his successor, Pianky, invaded in 720 BC, founding Egypt's Nubian twenty-fifth dynasty, which lasted until about 600 BC. Egypt then became subject successively to the Babylonians, the Persians, the Greeks, and the Romans.

By around 500 BC the Phoenician settlement and port of Carthage had become an independent state, but its glory did not last for long, and ultimately, after a series of wars, it was conquered by the Romans in 146 BC. Besides Egypt,

The Great Pyramid at Giza is perhaps the world's most recognizable building. Together with the other pyramids on the site, it was built over three generations by Khufu, Khafre, and Menkaure between 2723 and 2563 BC.

24

Roman settlement in North Africa was concentrated in two places: Tunisia, a province they called Africa, and Numidia. The Romans occupied all the arable land from Egypt to Mauretania (Morocco), which they garrisoned off from the marauding tribes and retained for nearly 500 years.

The penetration of Islam started with the Arab conquest of North Africa after the death of Prophet Mohammed in AD 632. The Arab invasion brought an end to Roman/Byzantine rule in Egypt, where the Coptic Church had become the chief source of resistance. Islam was spread by Arab nomads throughout the Sudan, and was withstood only by the Christian kingdoms in Nubia and Ethiopia. In the northwest, the Islamic Almoravid and the Almohad empires became two great trading states that spread their influence across the Mediterranean to Spain; rivalries fragmented these empires into a collection of small kingdoms. The Great Age of Islam lasted for about 400 years from AD 850.

From AD 900 to AD 1500, the kingdoms and empires of western and central Sudan were established in close proximity to the trans-Saharan trade routes. The empires of Ghana (800–1240), Mali (1240–1550), Bornu-Kanem (800–1700), and Songhay (1460–1600) along the strategic Niger River grew out of trading in slaves, ivory, gold, and kola nuts.

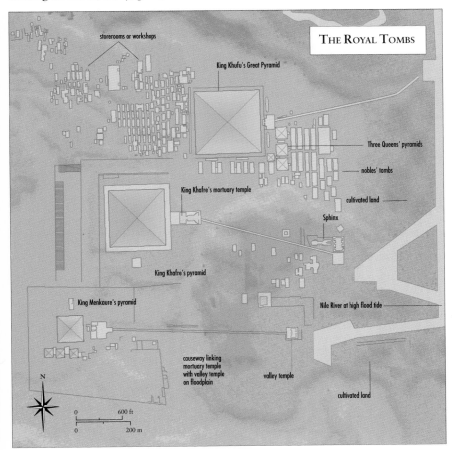

THE ROYAL TOMBS

storerooms or workshops

King Khufu's Great Pyramid

Three Queens' pyramids

nobles' tombs

King Khafre's mortuary temple

cultivated land

Sphinx

King Khafre's pyramid

King Menkaure's pyramid

Nile River at high flood tide

causeway linking mortuary temple with valley temple on floodplain

valley temple

cultivated land

N

0   600 ft

0   200 m

Songhay declined after conquest and occupation by the Moroccans in the late sixteenth century. Because of its strategic location in the Maghrib, between Europe and northern and western Africa, Morocco (Magreb Al Aksa) has constantly been a key player in the political and cultural changes of the region. Elsewhere, the Yoruba and the Ashanti maintained their independent economic prosperity, the latter especially thanks to their rich gold deposits. All these empires relied on large military organizations and sound administration and trade. The Hausa States were the single exception; although they were a loose confederation that never formed a political unit, they remained independent of larger empires while continuing to control the Niger Delta trade.

The Later Iron Age, between AD 1000 and 1500, was a period of change in the northeast. Pastoralists moved into the interior from the north, triggering a series of migrations, one effect of which was the formation of the Chwezi dynasty of Kitara (Bunyoro), with its capital at Bigo near the Katonga River in Uganda. Another lasting monument of this period is the finely engineered stone ruins of Great Zimbabwe.

In Egypt, the Mamelukes (1250–1517) built an economy based on agricultural production, taxation of the peasantry, and trade along the Red Sea between the Mediterranean and the Indian Ocean. In southern Africa the Karanga, a Shona people, built the Mwanamutapa empire south of the Zambezi around 1425, and, together with the Rowzi kingdom, they operated inland trade routes to the East African coast. West of the Niger Delta, the ancient cities of Benin and Ife reached their apogees around 1300.

Arab traders, as well as refugees from dynastic conflicts in the Middle East, spread Islam throughout East Africa, and by the twelfth century Shirazi Arabs had settled at Kilwa, and other important Arab coastal towns included Mombasa, Malindi, Mogadishu, and Zanzibar. Intermarriage between the Arab settlers, the native population, and immigrants of other origins created the present-day Swahili (Arabic for "coastal plain") culture. The Swahilis adopted Islam around AD 900, and their Kishwahili tongue became the national language of Uganda, Tanzania, and Kenya. It is widely spoken today in central and southern Africa.

Of the few animals adapted to life in the desert, the camel proved the most useful to man. This creature, once domesticated, became the key to trans-Saharan travel and occasional conquest.

THE OLD KINGDOM

The neolithic revolution entered Africa through Egypt, whose inhabitants had mastered the art of seasonal flooding to irrigate their crops using the waters of the Nile River. This settled way of life created the world's then most populated region, with a generally uniform culture gradually emerging along the whole length of the valley. Around 3100 BC, the previously separate red- and white-crowned kingdoms of the Upper (southern) and Lower (northern) Nile River were, if tradition is to be believed, united by King Menes, and Pharaonic dynasties began. Under their stable, centralized rule, Egyptian civilization began to flourish and expand, and Egyptian science, architecture, and hieroglyphic writing started to influence the neighboring states in Europe, northern Africa, western Asia, and to the south, especially in Nubia.

A cross-section of the pyramid of Giza, built by Khnum-Khuf (Khufu for short, or Cheops in Greek), rose to a hight of 481 feet (146.59 meters). It is said to contain 2.3 million blocks of stone, each weighing 2.5 tons.

The first four dynasties of Pharaohs are known as the Old Kingdom, and outstanding among them were Khufu, Khafre, and Menkaure, who built the early pyramids, including the Step pyramid at Saqqara, the oldest stone building in the world, and later the Great Pyramids at Giza, symbols of the Pharaohs' belief in god and the after-life, divine kingship, and earthly power.

Dependent on the ordinary people's labor, Egypt prospered in agriculture and trade with the surrounding countries of Africa and the Middle East. Trade and military expeditions were frequent, with Egypt extending its fortified southern borders into the Sudan, and its exploration and trade routes as far as Libya and western Asia. Harkuf, an outstanding Egyptian governor of the time, recorded his experiences on expeditions, which around 2300 BC took him to the Congo Basin. Since it made contacts with Africans south of the Sahara, and was bordered by Nubia, Egypt was always multicultural. Archaeological findings in the Nile Valley near the Aswan Dam show that pharaonic kingships were initiated by people who had migrated from the south.

The sixth dynasty under Pepi I saw a decentralization of power; Egypt began to decline, and experienced two centuries of breakdown exacerbated by warring princes and provinces, and by the constant threat of a rebellion amongst the poor. This accelerated the decline, for Egypt's prosperity depended on agricultural surpluses, and the period ended with the collapse of central authority.

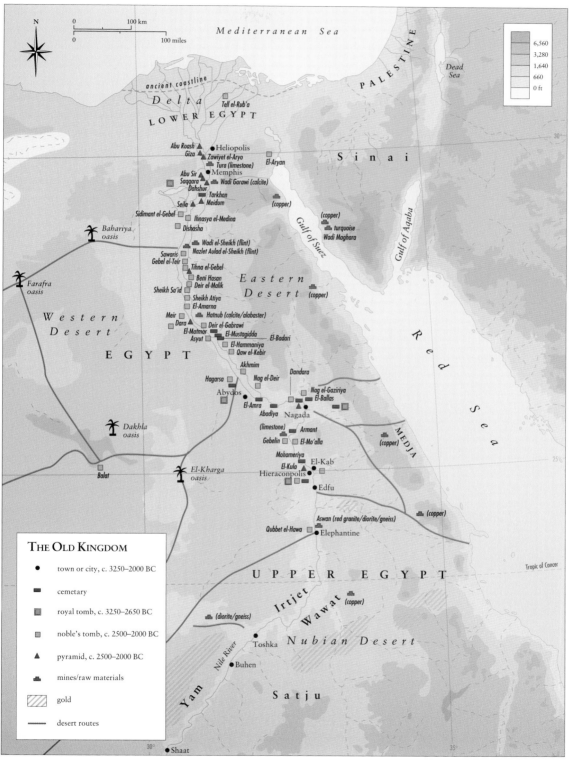

N

0   100 km

0   100 miles

Mediterranean Sea

PALESTINE

ancient coastline

Dead
Sea

D e l t a

LOWER EGYPT

Tell el-Rub'a

S i n a i

Abu Roash ▲ ● Heliopolis
Giza ▲
Zawiyet el-Aryo ▲
Tura (limestone)   El-Aryan
Abu Sir   ● Memphis
Saqqara   Wadi Garawi (calcite)
Dahshur
Tarkhan
Seila ▲ ▲ Meidum   (copper)

Sidimant el-Gebel   (copper)
Ihnasya el-Medina   turquoise
Dishasha   Wadi Maghara

Bahariya
oasis

Wadi el-Sheikh (flint)
Nazlet Aulad el-Sheikh (flint)
Sawaris   Tihna el-Gebel
Gebel el-Teir

E a s t e r n
D e s e r t

Farafra
oasis

Beni Hasan
Deir el-Malik
Sheikh Sa'id   Sheikh Atiya
El-Amarna   (copper)
W e s t e r n
D e s e r t   Meir   Hatnub (calcite/alabaster)
Dara ▲ Deir el-Gabrawi
El-Matmar   El-Mustagidda
E G Y P T   Asyut   El-Badari
El-Hammaniya
Qaw el-Kebir
Akhmim

Hagarsa   Nag el-Deir   Dandara

Abydos
El-Amra   Nag el-Gaziriya
Abadiya   El-Ballas
Nagada

R e d   S e a

Dakhla
oasis   (limestone)   Armant
Gebelin   El-Mo'alla   (copper)

MEDJA

Mohameriya
El-Kula   El-Kab
Hieraconpolis
El-Kharga
oasis   Edfu

(copper)

Balat

Aswan (red granite/diorite/gneiss)
Qubbet el-Hawa
● Elephantine

Tropic of Cancer

U P P E R   E G Y P T

Irtjet
Wawat   (copper)

(diorite/gneiss)

N u b i a n   D e s e r t

● Toshka

Nile River

● Buhen

Yam

S a t j u

● Shaat

THE OLD KINGDOM

● town or city, c. 3250–2000 BC

▬ cemetary

▣ royal tomb, c. 3250–2650 BC

▢ noble's tomb, c. 2500–2000 BC

▲ pyramid, c. 2500–2000 BC

⛏ mines/raw materials

▨ gold

— desert routes

30°

25°

35°

30°

35°

29

THE MIDDLE KINGDOM

From about 2000 BC the Middle Kingdom witnessed a revival of Egyptian fortunes. The founders of the Middle Kingdom came from Thebes in Upper Egypt, reestablished central unity and control by force of arms, and built new administrative centers. Taxes were collected efficiently, irrigation methods were revived, and more land was cultivated, the largest such project being at the Fayum Depression. It was a period of empire-building in which the power base shifted southward, as evidenced by the temples, palaces, pyramids, and tombs found along the southern corridor. Pharaohs like Inyoted, Mentuhotep I, and Ammenemes, who ruled at this time, conducted many military and commercial expeditions, especially into Nubia where gold was to be found, and the two lands of Egypt were once again reunited. Because of his personal abilities and the reorganization of Egypt's administration, Mentuhotep I was the most successful ruler of this period.

Pyramid building flourished once again, and trade routes expanded, reaching the Red Sea and East Africa. Menthuhotep II built the funerary temple at Deir el Bahari in Thebes, inaugurating a new architectural form. Amenemhet I, who succeeded him, established a new strategic capital at Ithet-Tawi, near El-Lisht, south of Memphis, from where he could rule Lower Egypt, while also establishing a trading center in the south to control Nubia and fortifying the trading post at Kerma, effectively controlling Nubia up to the Second Cataract. His successor, Senusret I, established a further fortified trading post at Buhen, and in about 1880 BC Senusret III finally captured all Nubia and made it an Egyptian province.

A guilded mummy mask from a burial at Thebes, made for a princess from the Dra Abu'l Naga region, attributed to the Middle Kingdom period.

The Middle Kingdom started to collapse, due to a series of weak rulers and fragmentation of local rule, and was brought to an end by the invasion of Egypt by the Hyksos from western Asia. For the first time Egypt was ruled by a foreign power with greater military might, especially in numbers of cavalry and chariots. The Hyksos introduced horses and armor, which later, in Egyptian hands, were to be turned on them. Around 1570 BC, Ahmose I united the Egyptians against the Hyksos; drove them from their capital, Avaris, into Palestine; and became founder of the eighteenth dynasty.

The Hyksos occupation was followed by a strong eighteenth dynasty at the start of the New Kingdom, in which Egyptian kings once again occupied Nubia, especially in the reign of Tuthmosis I. Ahmose's son, Amenhotep I, succeeded him and proved equally capable, conquering the rest of Nubia to the Third Cataract. Queen Hatshepsut (c. 1503–1482 BC) married each of her half brothers in turn, building two obelisks at the Karnak temple, but thwarted Tuthmosis III, who succeeded her, and who then attempted to erase all evidence of her reign. He extended the Egyptian empire to Palestine, Syria, and Lebanon, but was succeeded by kings who were satisfied to maintain the status quo.

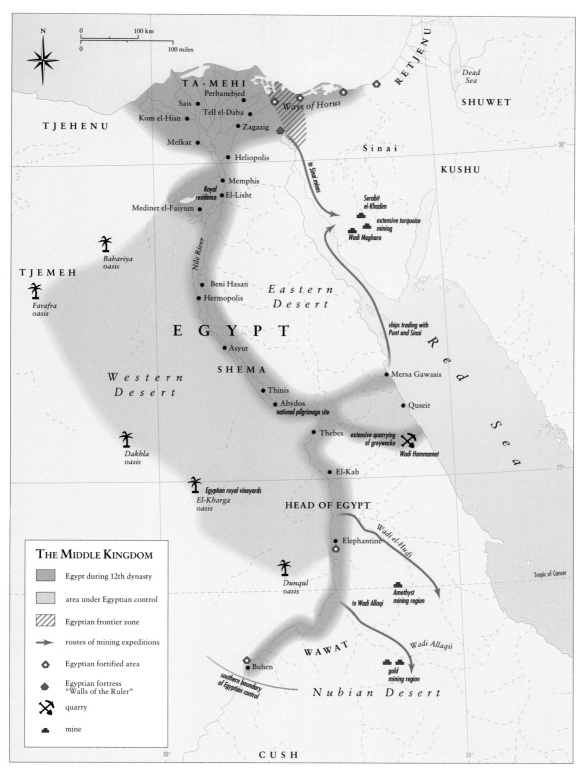

N

0   100 km
0   100 miles

TA-MEHI

TJEHENU

Perbanebjed
Sais
Tell el-Daba
Kom el-Hisn
Zagazig
Mefkat

Ways of Horus

Sinai

RETJENU

Dead Sea

SHUWET

KUSHU

Heliopolis

to Sinai mines

Memphis
Royal residence El-Lisht
Medinet el-Faiyum

Serabit el-Khadim
extensive turquoise mining
Wadi Maghara

Bahariya oasis

TJEMEH

Farafra oasis

Nile River

Beni Hasan
Hermopolis

Eastern Desert

E G Y P T

Asyut

Western Desert

SHEMA

Thinis
Abydos
national pilgrimage site

ships trading with Punt and Sinai

Mersa Gawasis

Quseir

R e d   S e a

Dakhla oasis

Thebes
extensive quarrying of greywacke
Wadi Hammamet

El-Kab

Egyptian royal vineyards
El-Kharga oasis

HEAD OF EGYPT

Wadi el-Hudi

Elephantine

Dunqul oasis

Tropic of Cancer

Amethyst mining region

to Wadi Allaqi

W A W A T

Wadi Allaqii

Buhen

southern boundary of Egyptian control

gold mining region

N u b i a n   D e s e r t

CUSH

THE MIDDLE KINGDOM

Egypt during 12th dynasty

area under Egyptian control

Egyptian frontier zone

routes of mining expeditions

Egyptian fortified area

Egyptian fortress "Walls of the Ruler"

quarry

mine

31

THE NEW KINGDOM

The Ramesseum or morturary complex of Pharaoh Rameses II at Medinet Habu.

The New Kingdom's next powerful ruler was to be Amenophis III, whose lasting achievements are the Luxor temple and other large buildings at Karnak and throughout the empire. He started the cult of Aten, and his succeeding son, Amenophis IV, attacked the traditional priesthood of Amun. In reaction to the wrath of his people he built a new capital at El-Amarna in Middle Egypt, which he called Akhet-Aten. In order to restore religious unity, the boy-king Tut-Ankh-Aten changed his name back to Tut-Ankh-Amun, while in practice his co-regent, Semenekh-Ka-Re, ruled the country. Tutankhamun formally held office for about nine years, dying at the age of eighteen.

The nineteenth dynasty started with Horemheb after the death of Tutankhamun and the short reign of King Ay. He strengthened the kingdom by suppressing corruption and introducing the collection of a national tax. However, after Horemheb, Kings Rameses I and II were troubled by attacks from Syria and Libya. Rameses II moved the capital to Pi-Ramesse in the northeastern region of the Nile Delta.

This period witnessed the reestablishment of a greater Egypt with a strong standing army. Palestine, Syria, and Nubia were reconquered, and the Egyptian capital was established at Thebes in Upper Egypt. Trade routes expanded through the Red Sea to northeastern Africa (Somalia), and the tradition of building great temples, tombs, and statues restarted.

The New Kingdom Egyptianized Nubia, with the eighteenth and nineteenth dynasties in particular building numerous temples around which towns developed. The campaign aimed to enlist the support of local Nubian chieftains, while Egyptian scribes, soldiers, priests, artisans, and architects lived among the people and taught them to worship the Egyptian gods. Egypt in turn depended on Nubian wealth in grain, oils, cattle, giraffes, ostrich feathers, wood, ebony, ivory, incense, carnelian, hematite, malachite, slaves, and, above all, gold, which came from Wadi Allaqi and Wadi Gabgada in the east and from mines along the Nile. Nubia became crucial to Egypt's survival as a state because of its wealth and its strong army. Whenever internal conflict arose in Egypt, its contenders would seek the support of Nubia.

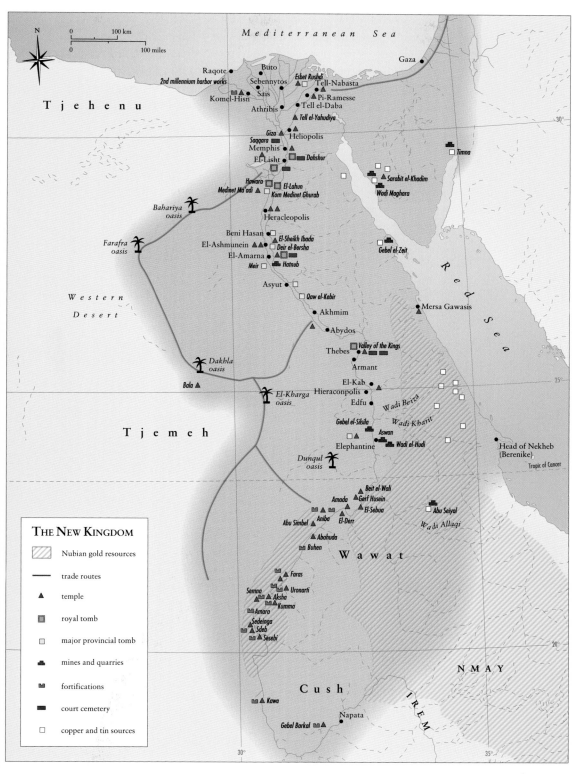

N

0   100 km
0   100 miles

Mediterranean Sea

Gaza

T j e h e n u

Raqote
Buto
2nd millennium harbor works
Sebennytos
Esbet Rushdi
Tell-Nabasta
Sais
Pi-Ramesse
Komel-Hisn
Tell el-Daba
Athribis
Tell el-Yahudiya

30°

Giza
Heliopolis
Saqqara
Memphis
Timna
El-Lisht
Dahshur
Sarabit el-Khadim
Hawara
El-Lahun
Wadi Maghara
Medinet Ma'adi
Kom Medinet Ghurab
Bahariya oasis

Heracleopolis

Farafra oasis
Beni Hasan
El-Sheikh Ibada
El-Ashmunein
Deir el-Bersha
Gebel el-Zeit
El-Amarna
Meir
Hatnub

Western Desert
Asyut
Qaw el-Kebir

Akhmim
Mersa Gawasis

Abydos

Dakhla oasis
Thebes
Valley of the Kings
Bala
Armant

25°

El-Kab
Hieraconpolis
El-Kharga oasis
Edfu
Wadi Beiza

Gebel el-Silsila
T j e m e h
Wadi Kharit
Aswan
Elephantine
Wadi el-Hudi
Dunqul oasis
Head of Nekheb
(Berenike)
Tropic of Cancer

R e d   S e a

Beit el-Wali
Amada
Gerf Husein
El-Sebua
Abu Seiyal
Abu Simbel
Aniba
El-Derr
Wadi Allaqi

Abahuda

Buhen
W a w a t

Faras
Semna
Uronarti
Aksha
Kumma
Amara
Sedeinga
Sdeb
Sesebi

20°

N M A Y

C u s h

Kawa
I R E M
Napata
Gebel Barkal

THE NEW KINGDOM

▨ Nubian gold resources

⎯ trade routes

▲ temple

▣ royal tomb

□ major provincial tomb

♣ mines and quarries

⊔ fortifications

▬ court cemetery

□ copper and tin sources

30°   35°

THE KINGDOM OF CUSH

The face detail of a granite sphinx, from the temple of Kawa in Nubia. The features represent King Taharqa of the twenty-fifth dynasty.

The histories of Egypt and the rest of Africa are entangled, and they share numerous common artistic, cultural, and religious heritages. Nubia, the land immediately to the south of Egypt (present-day northern Sudan), had a civilization that was thriving by the seventeenth century BC, and which reached its peak with the Cushite kingdom around 600 BC. The region was rich in gold; its people built forts and temples and founded trading cities; and it formed the most important corridor between Egypt and Africa south of the Sahara.

Under the rule of the Libyan twenty-second and twenty-third dynasties, Egypt enjoyed initial success, only to suffer eventual fragmentation and disunity spurred by ethnic rivalry between Upper and Lower Egypt. In the north, Tefnakht, from his power base at Sais, rose to unite the Delta and establish the twenty-fourth dynasty. To the south, the ruling family of Napata emerged as the leaders of a united Cushite kingdom. Styling themselves as traditional pharoahs, the Cushites sought to extend their control over the whole of Egypt. Tefnakht organized a coalition to oppose this move. King Kashata led the first Nubian military expedition northward against Egypt in 750 BC. Pianky (alternatively translated Peye, or Piy), his successor in 730 BC, invaded Egypt in about 728 BC. Through strict discipline and religious observance, Pianky was able to galvanize his forces, conquer local Libyan chiefs, unite Egypt, and impose an administration that lasted for sixty years, until the invasion of the Assyrians.

His reign, founding the twenty-fifth dynasty, is well recorded on the inscribed Stelae of Victory, whose hieroglyphs recount the war against the Libyans in detail. Pianky was succeeded in 716 BC by his brother Shabaka, who brought the whole of the Nile Valley under the control of the Cush empire, prompting the construction of monuments throughout the territory. Shabaka was succeeded by Pianky's sons Shabataka (700–690 BC) and Taharqa (690–664 BC). The latter built numerous shrines in the kingdom, erected temples at the foot of Jebel Barkal Mountain, and constructed colonnades at the Temple of Karnak. It was probably because of the influence of priests at the Jebel Barkal temple that the Cushites became Egyptianized.

There had already begun a period of military conflict with the Assyrians, who in 663 BC, in the reign of Tautimani, invaded, occupied, and plundered Thebes. With the Assyrian conquest of Thebes, the Nubians' control over Egypt ended, and they were forced to withdraw southward.

Nubia never again ventured to the north, and some 150 years later, Egypt was overrun in 525 BC by the Persians. Nubia moved its capital farther south, from Napata to Meroe.

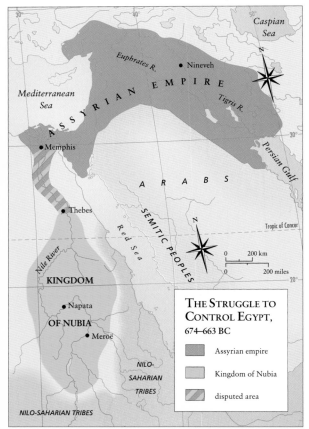

THE STRUGGLE TO CONTROL EGYPT, 674–663 BC

Assyrian empire

Kingdom of Nubia

disputed area

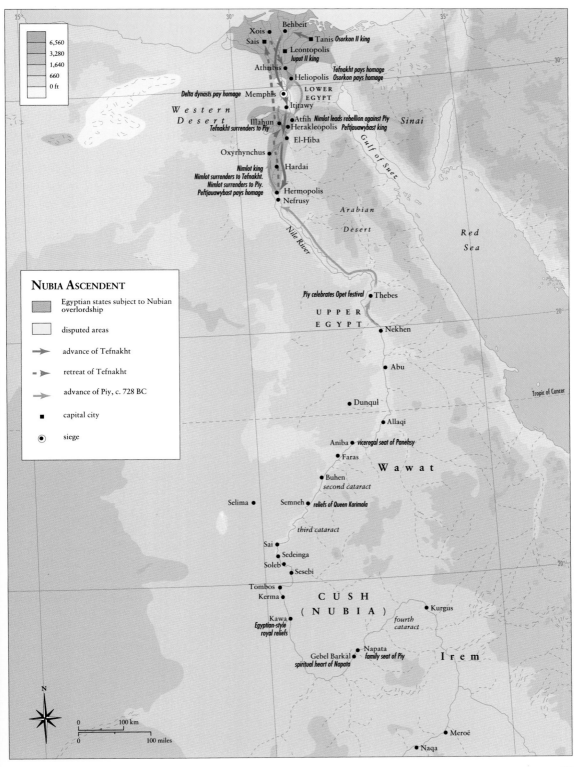

Xois ■ Behbeit

Sais ■   ● Tanis *Osorkon II king*

■ Leontopolis
  Iuput II king

Athribis ●
              Tefnakht pays homage
  ● Heliopolis   *Osorkon pays homage*

Delta dynasts pay homage Memphis ◉ **LOWER**
                                      EGYPT
                          ● Itjtawy

                    ● Atfih *Nimlot leads rebellion against Piy*
Illahun ●   Herakleopolis ● *Peftjauawybast king*
Tefnakht surrenders to Piy

          ● El-Hiba

Oxyrhynchus ●

Nimlot king
Nimlot surrenders to Tefnakht.   ● Hardai
Nimlot surrenders to Piy.
Peftjauawybast pays homage
                          ● Hermopolis
                          ● Nefrusy

Western Desert

Sinai

Gulf of Suez

Arabian
Desert

Red
Sea

Nile River

Piy celebrates Opet festival ● Thebes

UPPER
EGYPT
              ● Nekhen

          ● Abu

Tropic of Cancer

          ● Dunqul

              ● Allaqi

Aniba ● *viceregal seat of Panehsy*

    ● Faras   **W a w a t**

    ● Buhen
    second cataract

Selima ●   Semneh ● *reliefs of Queen Karimala*

    third cataract

Sai ●
  ● Sedeinga
Soleb ●
      ● Sesebi

Tombos ●
Kerma ●   **C U S H**
        (N U B I A)   ● Kurgus
                        fourth
                        cataract
Kawa ●
Egyptian-style
royal reliefs
              ● Napata
Gebel Barkal ● *family seat of Piy*   **I r e m**
spiritual heart of Napata

              ● Meroë

          ● Naqa

NUBIA ASCENDENT

Egyptian states subject to Nubian overlordship

disputed areas

→ advance of Tefnakht

⇢ retreat of Tefnakht

→ advance of Piy, c. 728 BC

■ capital city

◉ siege

6,560
3,280
1,640
660
0 ft

N

0 — 100 km
0 — 100 miles

ROMAN AFRICA

With its conquest of Phoenician Carthage after the battle of Zama in the third Punic War, Rome gained control of North Africa and became the dominant imperial power, with a large overseas empire. To achieve total control of the region, the Romans razed Carthage in 146 BC, made Tunisia and Egypt Roman provinces, and occupied Numidia. During the last century BC Roman attention focused on Egypt, and after a series of treaties, it became fully incorporated into the empire. Egypt provided the Roman empire with its agricultural wealth, especially its grain and papyrus products, and a strategic position astride the trade routes with the Middle East, Asia, and the Indian Ocean.

Berber nomads from Tripolitania and Cyrenaica frequently raided Roman settlements along the edge of the Sahara, sometimes going as far as the Libyan coast and the Egyptian oases. In order to ward off these raids, the Romans occupied the agricultural lands of the Maghrib, bordering the Sahara. Garrisons of soldiers guarded the frontier zone (the limes) and built networks of forts and roads. Typical of the the many Roman foundations in North Africa is Timgad.

There were several Roman-Berber wars, the best known of which is the Tacfarinas campaign, fought by Emperor Tiberius for eight years over most of North Africa. The Berber king of Numidia had intended to reduce by half the Roman territories, which he saw as his people's birthright, but in the end Roman rule was secured. As a result a new race of Romano-Berbers steadily evolved.

The Julio-Claudian emperors extended Roman power from Cirta in the west to Tacape in the south, and the Flavian emperors extended it to Sitifis. However,

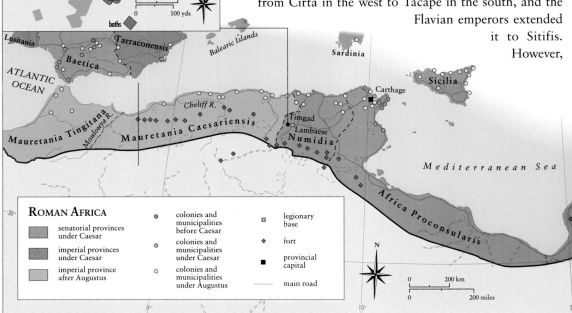

36

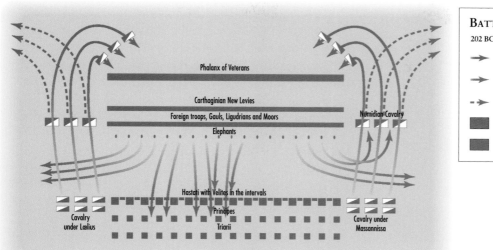

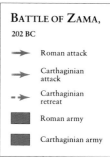

BATTLE OF ZAMA,
202 BC

→ Roman attack

→ Carthaginian attack

⇢ Carthaginian retreat

▬ Roman army

▬ Carthaginian army

Phalanx of Veterans

Carthaginian New Levies

Foreign troops, Gauls, Ligudrians and Moors

Elephants

Numidian Cavalry

Hastati with Velites in the intervals

Cavalry under Lœlius

Principes

Triarii

Cavalry under Massannissa

despite Roman military might, nomads continued to cross the borders to attack their trade caravans and settlements.

Roman North Africa was ruled by a Senate-appointed governor whose duties included the maintenance of a steady supply of corn to Rome and the supervision of the fiscal system. Life in Roman Africa was highly civilized, and by the end of the Romans' reign they had established over five hundred cities.

Colonnades at Sabratha on the coast of Lybia, a once prosperous town and port, supporting two theatres, temples, and public baths.

VANDALS AND BYZANTINES

Justinian, Byzantian emperor from AD 527. He was determined to recapture lost Roman territories. This included North Africa.

When in AD 428, the migrating Germanic tribe known as the Vandals, led by the ruthless King Gaiseric, invaded northwestern Africa with the intention of capturing and controlling the African grain trade to Europe, Roman North Africa stretched along the Mediterranean coast from Morocco in the west to Egypt in the east.

The Vandals' onslaught came at a time when the empire was also suffering internal conflict and incursions by other barbarian tribes, and it was in irreversible decline. Entering North Africa via the Straits of Gibraltar, the Vandals landed at Ceuta, captured Hippone in 430, and by 439 gained complete control of Constantine and Carthage, which became their capital. The Romans, however, still held on in Western Numidia, Mauretania Caesariensis, and Mauritania Sitifensis.

The Vandals retained the Romans' administrative and agrarian methods, but apart from Ammaedara, Theveste, and Hippone, the towns began to depopulate and decay under the new regime. Unfettered by the Vandals or Romans, the local Moorish tribal kingdoms of Baquates, Masuna, Djeddar, Hodna, Aures, Capsus, Grande Dorsale, and Cabaon thrived and would later contribute to the collapse of the Vandals' thriving grain empire.

Internally the Vandals' oppression of the Christian clergy was excessive, and in 533 the Byzantine emperor Justinian (527–565), driven by his own desire to rebuild the Roman empire, ordered his army, led by General Belisarius, to attack. Within three months the

Map

Tagus R.

Guadiana R.

SPAIN

Guadalquivir R.

Balearic Islands

Sardinia

Cartagena

Septum
Tingi • Ceuta

Portus Magnus

Rusguniae
Caesarea
Saldae
Rusicadae

Hippo Regius

Decimum
Carthage

Sicily

Syracuse

Taza

KINGDOM
OF MASUNA
IN ORAN • Altava

DJEDDAR

Djeddar

Cheliff R.

HODNA
Cirta

NUMIDIA

Tricamarum

Thugga

Malta

Moulouya R.

AURES
NEMENCHA

GRANDE
DORSALE

B
Y
Z
CAPSUS
A
N
TRIPOLITANIA
T
I
N

Sabratha

Oea (Trip

CABAON

Leptis Magna

BYZANTINE AFRICA AND INDIGENOUS KINGDOMS, 565–600

☐ Roman Byzantine empire

☐ indigenous kingdoms

CAPSUS indigenous state

N

0   200 km

0   200 miles

Vandals had lost almost all their territory. With the edict of 534, the Byzantines restructured the administration of the region along legal and military lines, then embarked on the reconquest of the eastern Maghrib, a task made difficult by the indigenous mountain kingdoms. Fortresses had to be constructed to protect the Byzantine line of supply and agricultural areas from attacks by surrounding tribes, and their empire was confined to the coastal strip of Caesarea, Rusguniae, Cartenna, and Tipasa. Ceuta, surrounded by Berber kingdoms, was an isolated western possession of the Byzantines, who remained in control until 639, when invading Islamic Arab armies overan Egypt and North Africa.

THE VANDALS IN AFRICA, 435–533

Vandal invasion, 429–431

Vandal seaborne raids

Vandal empire at its maximum extent, c. 450

CAPSUS   indigenous state

Corsica

Rome
sacked 455

OSTROGOTHS

Sardinia

SPAIN

VISIGOTHS

Balearic Islands

Mediterranean Sea

Sicily

Caesarea

Saldae

Rusicadae

Hippo Regius

Syracuse

Portus Magnus

MAURETANIA CAESARIENSIS

Cirta

PROCONSULARIS

Carthage

Taza

KINGDOM OF MASUNA IN ORAN

Altava

DJEDDAR

HODNA
MAURETANIA SITIFIENSIS

NUMIDIA

AURES NEMENCHA

BYZACENA

GRANDE DORSALE

CAPSUS

Malta

Sabratha

Oea (Tripoli)

TRIPOLITANIA

CABAON

Leptis Magna

N

0   200 km

0   200 miles

Cyprus

Crete

Mediterranean Sea

Jerusalem

M   P   I   R   E

Cyrene

Pelusium

Berenice

LIBYA PENTAPOLIS (CYRENAICA)

LIBYA INFERIOR

Alexandria

Naucratis

1

2   4

3

EGYPT

Aila

Memphis

1   AEGYPTUS I

2   AEGYPTUS II

3   AUGUSTAMNICA I

4   AUGUSTAMNICA II

ARCADIA

Nile River

THEBAIS INFERIOR

THE EMPIRES OF GHANA AND MALI

> "I hired a guide
> from the
> Messufah tribe.
> There is no need
> whatever to
> travel in large
> groups, since
> the route is very
> safe.
> I departed with
> three men, and
> all along the
> road we found
> great, hundred-
> year-old trees.
> One of them
> alone affords
> enough shade
> for a whole
> caravan."
> *Ibn Battutta,*
> Arab traveler,
> West Africa,
> c. 1354

*A detail (far right) from
a Catalan map drawn
c. 1375 shows an African
king enthroned, possibly
Mansa Musa
of Mali.*

Ancient Ghana was one of the Early Iron Age communities of western Africa, and the language of its inhabitants, the Soninke, belongs to the Niger-Congo group. It was situated between the Sahara in the north and the Senegal and Niger rivers in the south, and was rich in gold. Its rulers controlled trade in the region and had influence that extended eastward to Sudan.

The Ghanian empire originated as a coalition of ironworking and agricultural communities that combined to form a larger kingdom. Ghana's proximity to the Saharan trading links provided horses, and these, together with iron-headed weapons, gave the Soninke a decisive trading and military advantage over their neighbors. With their thriving trade and income from the Wangara and Bambuk goldfields, the capital at Kumbi-Saleh prospered, and the Soninke maintained a strong, well-equipped army. At the empire's height, around AD 1050, the Soninke occupied Awdaghust, a Berber trading stronghold to the north.

As early as the eighth century, Ghana's fame had been recorded in the Arabic geographical writings of Ibn Battutta and Al Fazari. At his court, the King of Ghana employed Islamic officials, secretaries, and ministers to keep accounts of his trade and business, and Al-Bakri, who traveled to Ghana in AD 1067, wrote about the magnificence of the ancient city, noting that it was divided into one part for Africans and another for Muslim emigrants and traders; he described King Tunka Manin as the powerful ruler of a great empire.

Conflicts between the Soninke and the Almoravids were affecting the trans-Saharan trade, and in 1055 the Sanhaja Berbers retook Awdaghust, a precursor to conquering and occupying Ghana itself in 1076. By the twelfth century the Ghanaian empire was in decline.

Most of the gold dealers who had traded with the Ghanian kings were Mandinka from Wangara. At around the beginning of the thirteenth century, new gold mines were discovered at Bure in the upper Niger River area. This led to active participation in the trans-Saharan trade by the southern Soninke and Malinke people, inspiring them to rebel, hastening the final disintegration of the Ghanian empire, and generating the rise of a new kingdom at Sosso. Its rulers, especially Sumaguru, killed and pillaged the surrounding states of the Malinke and Soninke. Resistance to the Sosso was organized by Sundjata, a Malinke who reunited Malinke chiefdoms against Sumaguru, defeating him in 1235. Sundjata then exercised his control over the Soninke to form a great new empire known as Mali, whose capital was Niani near the goldfields of Bure. Having persuaded the remaining Malinke chiefs to surrender their *mansa* (titles) to him, Sundjata became both religious and secular leader of his people. Other important trading towns of the Mali empire were Jenne, Walata, Tadmekka, and Gao; Timbuktu, also an important cultural center, developed as a result of the discovery of the Akan goldfields.

Mali became famous for its wealth, its stability, and its scholars. Although it only lasted for about two centuries, at its height it was the most influential state in western Sudan. Malian rulers were all devout Muslims. Mansa Kankan Musa

(1312–1337) reigned at the empire's height and is remembered for his sensational pilgrimage in 1324 to Mecca, where he displayed his immense wealth in gold. Ibn Battutta, an Arab traveler who visited Mali in 1352 during the reign of Mansa Sulayman (1341–1360), noted the splendor of the empire and the great peace and order that prevailed there.

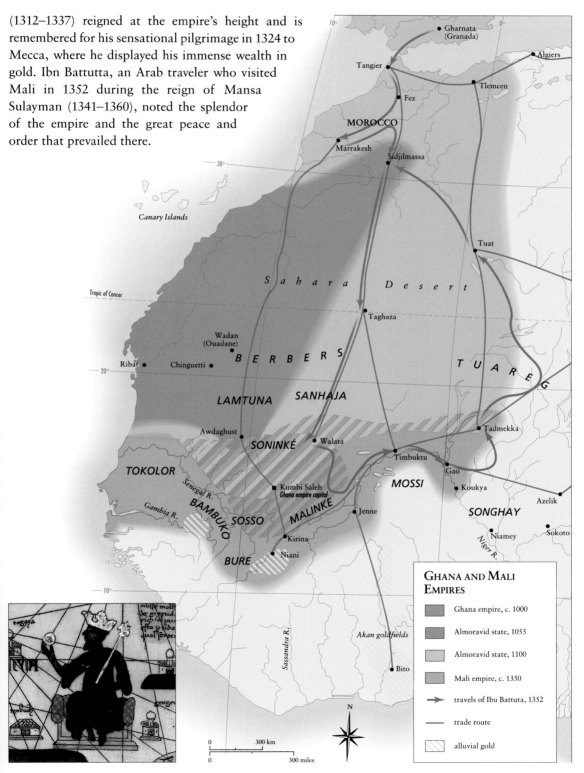

GHANA AND MALI EMPIRES

- Ghana empire, c. 1000
- Almoravid state, 1055
- Almoravid state, 1100
- Mali empire, c. 1350
- → travels of Ibu Battuta, 1352
- — trade route
- alluvial gold

41

THE BERBER BROTHERHOOD

The Maghrib is the area of northwestern Africa located around the Atlas Mountains that includes present-day Morocco (also known as Magreb Al Aksa), Algeria, Libya, and Tunisia. Today its people are of mixed descent, from the Mediterranean countries, Arabia, and the Middle East, but the region's original African inhabitants were the Berbers. The Berbers lived in three different locations: the agriculturalists along the Mediterranean coast known as Bilad e Makhzen (the Land of Order), and the nomadic Sanhaja, Masmuda, and Zenata in the Atlas Mountains and in the borders of the Sahara called Bilal es Siba (the Land of Disobedience).

Because of their different terrains and distinct cultures, the Berber kingdoms were independent and free from any central control. They learned metalworking skills from Spain and the East, and spread southward, some as far as southern Sudan. Most, however, remained in the Maghrib, and only those who were traders and settled in towns were able to form strong kingdoms. Using horse-drawn chariots, they opened trade routes across the Sahara to Sudan, Morocco, Tunisia, and western Libya, bringing great prosperity to the Phoenician city of Carthage. The Carthaginian merchants forged strong links with the Berbers, from whom they bought gold and a variety of goods transported from the sub-Saharan interior.

When the Romans fought and defeated the Carthaginians in the Punic Wars, they took control of the Berber states along the coast, conquering and occupying them until the invasion of Islamized Germanic Vandals in AD 428. It was the Romans who introduced camels from Asia and taught the Berbers to use them to cross the desert, expanding their trade and in turn creating more Berber states. The southernmost of these established links with West African traders like the Soninke, who later formed the empire of Ghana.

By AD 705 the Arabs had completely conquered the Maghrib from present-day Morocco in the west to the land of the Sanhaja Berbers in the south. By this time the Sanhaja were already trading with western Sudan, Senegal, and Ghana, a source of gold. Other Sanhaja routes led from western Algeria to central Niger and from Tripolitania to Lake Chad, Songhay, and Mali.

Islam united the Berbers, gave them a sense of common brotherhood, and inspired their attack on the Sudanese nonbelievers who inhabited the Sahel. A Sanhaja chief who traveled to Mecca invited a Muslim scholar, Abdallah ibn Yasin, to return with him and reform the faith among the Sanhaja Berbers, and to convert the Sudanese. Abdallah ibn Yasin, in his attempt to convert the Juddala Sanhaja, recruited a group of the faithful, known as al-Murabitun or Almoravids, "the men of the monastery," whom he trained in strict religious and military skills to conduct jihads (holy wars). They inspired the Sanhaja Berbers to rebel and become independent. Converted into a Muslim sect run on military lines, the Sanhaja state began to expand.

The western Berbers united Morocco around 1056, and made Marrakesh its capital in 1070. The Lamtuna Sanhaja Berbers joined the religious movement against the Soninke and others in the Western Sahara. Here the main participants were two brothers, Yahya ibn Umar and

A good war justifies any cause.
Berber saying

Abu-Bakr, who liberated and converted two important trading towns along the western trans-Saharan routes (Sajilmasa in the north in 1054, and Soninke-held Awdaghust in the south in 1055).

To maintain control over the gained territory the group split, with Abu-Bakr going south to conquer Ghana, Songhay, and Sudan (1076–1083), and his cousin Yusuf ibn Tashufin ruling Morocco and expanding into southern Spain and western Algeria (1082). From their northern city, Marrakesh, the Almoravids controlled the whole of the western Maghrib and beyond.

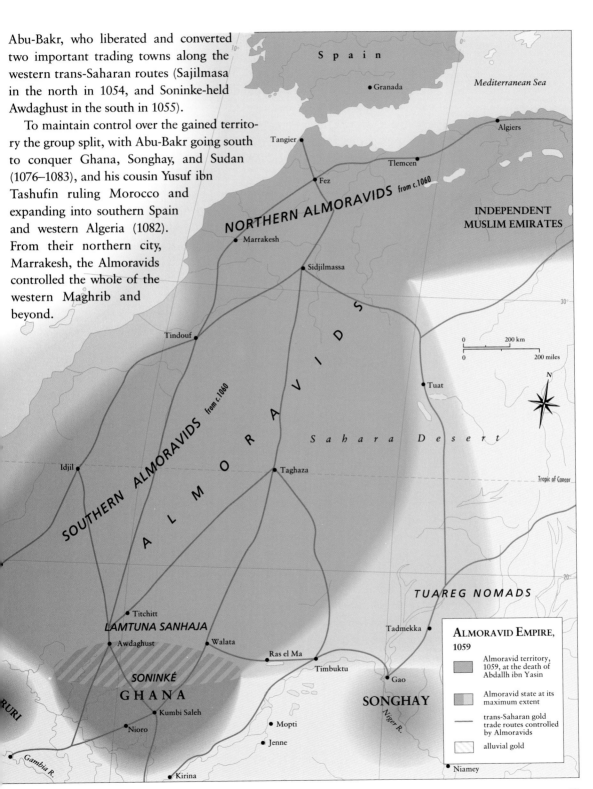

ALMORAVID EMPIRE, 1059

Almoravid territory, 1059, at the death of Abdallh ibn Yasin

Almoravid state at its maximum extent

trans-Saharan gold trade routes controlled by Almoravids

alluvial gold

EGYPT, 640–1517

Egypt became predominantly Muslim after the Arab invasion of AD 639, although it was not until three centuries or so later that Islam almost completely obliterated Christianity. From Egypt, Islam spread across North Africa and to northern Sudan and became the religion of the new Funj Sultanate.

With the growth of Islam came determined Arab and Berber leaders who invaded and occupied states in Europe and North Africa, spreading their faith and bringing education, political stability, economic growth, and unity. The Fatimids (descendants of Fatima, Prophet Mohammed's daughter), who occupied and ruled Egypt from 969 to 1171, depended on the Berbers for their conquest of the desert lands. When in 973 Fatimid caliph Al-Mu'izz moved his capital from the Maghrib to Cairo (al-Cahira), he lost control of the Maghrib to the Sanhaja chiefs, who created the kingdoms in Tunisia and Algeria around 1014–1049.

The Fatimid caliphate of Egypt built up a large trading empire, which massively developed trans-Saharan trade. The Fatimid dinar (minted in gold imported from the grassland states of western Africa) became the standard of exchange throughout the region. The Fatimids had depended on a largely Berber army, part of which was also composed of Mamelukes (Turkish slave horsemen) and Sudanese slaves. Widespread rebellions in 1050 were suppressed with the help of the Bedouins, in the form of raids launched by two tribes, the Banu Hilal along the coast and the Banu Sulayman inland.

Salah al-Din (Saladin), the Mameluke general who repulsed the Christian Crusaders, took over as ruler after the death of the last Fatimid caliph in 1171. Salah al-Din founded the Ayyubid dynasty, presiding over a period of Egyptian prosperity that saw increased agricultural production, expanded trade along the Red Sea between the Mediterranean and the Indian Ocean, and organized taxation of the peasantry. In 1250 the Mamelukes killed the last Ayyubid sultan and took over the reins of power, ruling Egypt until 1517.

This illustration from the Book of Knowledge of Mechanical Devices shows a candle surrounded by doors. An hour after the wick is lit, a ball falls from the falcon's beak, opening a door from which a figurine emerges. From the Mameluke period, Egypt.

The Mamelukes ruled the most powerful Muslim empire, extending to Palestine, Syria, and the holy cities of Medina and Mecca. They ruled Egypt as a military dictatorship, and the Red Sea trade route prospered, with gold and emeralds being mined in the Aswan Mountains, and public works and agricultural developments being completed with the use of peasant labor.

In the same period, Arabs spread from Egypt into the Maghrib, where, apart from a few isolated tribes, their language and culture were absorbed by the inhabitants of the region.

The Mamelukes declined mainly because their wealthy rulers abandoned militarism, and the population was ravaged by the Black Death—reducing taxation by 1517 to one-fifth of that collected in 1315—and leaving the sultan to finance a standing army through direct taxation. This weakened condition allowed the Ottoman Turks to conquer Egypt in 1517. In the Upper Nile, Amars Dunkas allied with Abdullab, an important Arab sheikh, to conquer the Christian kingdoms and unite them in a Muslim sultanate, the Funj.

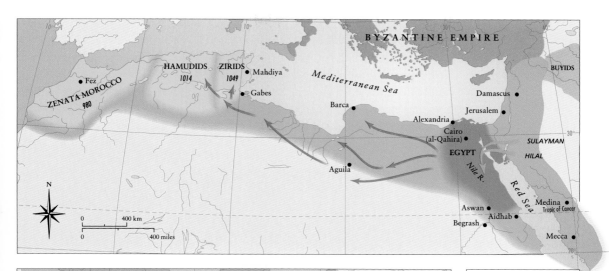

BYZANTINE EMPIRE

BUYIDS

HAMUDIDS   ZIRIDS   • Mahdiya
1014   1049

• Fez   Mediterranean Sea

ZENATA MOROCCO   • Gabes   • Damascus
980
                                      • Barca   Jerusalem •

                                          Alexandria •
                                                      Cairo •   SULAYMAN
                                                   (al-Qahira)   HILAL
                                                      EGYPT

                                                         Nile R.

N   Red Sea
                                      • Aguila   • Medina
                                                                                Tropic of Cancer
0   400 km

0   400 miles   • Aswan
                                                 • Aidhab
                                   • Begrash
                                                                          • Mecca

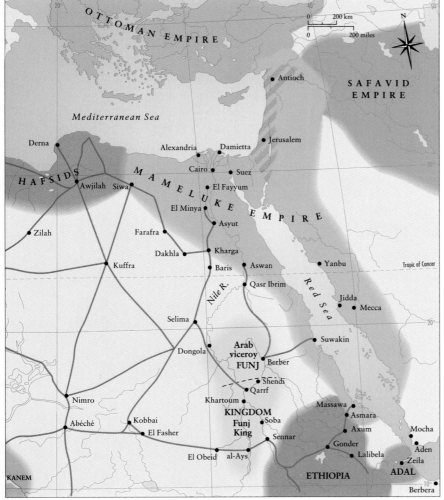

OTTOMAN EMPIRE   0   200 km   N

                                                         0   200 miles

                          • Antioch   SAFAVID
                                                 EMPIRE
Mediterranean Sea

• Derna   Alexandria •   Damietta •   Jerusalem •

HAFSIDS   • Awjilah Siwa •   Cairo •   Suez •
        M A M E L U K E
• Zilah   El Fayyum •
                         E M P I R E
                                      El Minya •

• Kuffra   Farafra •   Asyut •

                 Dakhla •   Kharga •
                          Baris • Aswan •   • Yanbu   Tropic of Cancer
                                      Qasr Ibrim •
                                                      Red Sea
                                                         • Jidda
                 • Selima   • Mecca

                    • Dongola
                                      • Suwakin
              Arab
• Nimro   viceroy
              FUNJ   Berber •
                          Shendi •
• Abéché   Qarrf •
        Kobbai •   Khartoum •   Massawa •
          El Fasher •   • Asmara   • Mocha
              KINGDOM   • Axum
              Funj   Soba •   • Aden
              King   Sennar •   • Zeila
        El Obeid • al-Ays •   Gonder •
                                   • Lalibela
KANEM   ETHIOPIA   ADAL
                                                      • Berbera

FATIMID NORTH
AFRICA TO c. 1000

Fatimid caliphate
at its maximum
extent, c. 1000

breakaway
principalities,
with date

movement of Arab
peoples (Banu Hilal
and Banu Sulayman),
c. 1000

Fatimid caliphate,
c. 1055

Sulayman and Hilal
attacks, encouraged
by the Fatimids

MAMELUKE
SULTANATE, 1171–1517

Mameluke territory,
c. 1400

territory recaptured
by the Mameluke
from European
crusaders by 1291

trade route

THE SONGHAY EMPIRE

The cemetery at Gao, the burial place of Askia Mohammed, ruler of the Songhay empire from 1493 to 1528.

Songhay came to prominence as the principal state of Mali. Situated in its easternmost province, it lay along the Niger River bend. Its people controlled the fishing all along the river. For the rulers of Mali, Songhay was of strategic importance, as it afforded direct access to Timbuktu and Gao, but the nobles of Songhay detested Mali's control of their land. Sonni Ali (1464–1492) became the most prominent Songhay ruler. He fought and defeated Mali. Ali spent his reign suppressing revolts from among his own Mande people as well as fighting the surrounding Tuareg, Mossi, and Fulani clans. He captured Timbuktu from the Tuareg in 1468, and established trade routes with capitals in Timbuktu, Jenne, and Gao.

Ali's successor, Askia Mohammed Turre (1493–1528), founder of the Turre dynasty, established his capital at Gao, east of Niani. Besides spreading Islam, Askia Mohammed extended the empire to the borders of Morocco in the north, as far as Bornu in the east, and beyond Walata in the west. He established control over the Tuareg of Takedda and Air, captured the salt deposits of Taghaza, and tightened his hold over trans-Saharan trade. He declared a jihad (holy war) against the Mossi and raided them in 1498.

On his return from Mecca he rebuilt Timbuktu to its former glory as a center of Islamic scholarship. During his strong reign, Songhay was enriched by taxes on trade, tribute from its provinces, and exports of gold, kola nuts, and slaves.

The decline of Songhay in the late sixteenth century, and its occupation by Morocco, witnessed the shift of power over the trans-Saharan trade routes to the eastern Sudanic kingdom of Bornu-Kanem and the Hausa states. This period also saw the arrival of European traders on the West African coast, a factor that persuaded the Akan gold traders to move southward. Kanem, northeast of Lake Chad, came into existence around 900, and reached the height of its power under Mai Dunama Dibalemi (1210–1248). Its Kanuri inhabitants were nomadic pastoralists who became wealthy through control of the central Saharan routes passing through Kanem to Fezzan, Tripoli, and Egypt. Their main trading commodities were ostrich feathers, slaves captured in raids on neighboring states, and ivory. Bornu was a tributary state of Kanem until the thirteenth century, when the latter declined and Bornu strengthened. Sultan Idris Aloma, using musketeers, subdued Kanem at the beginning of the seventeenth century. At about this time the Hausa states of Kano, Katsina, Zaria, and Gobir also became important political players in the region.

Canary Is.

Tropic of Cancer

Idjil

Arguin

Chinguetti

St. Louis

Kaédi

Senegal R.

DIA

Gorée

Gambia R.

Kayes

Kit

Cacheu

Bissau

MALI

Pita

K

kola, slaves

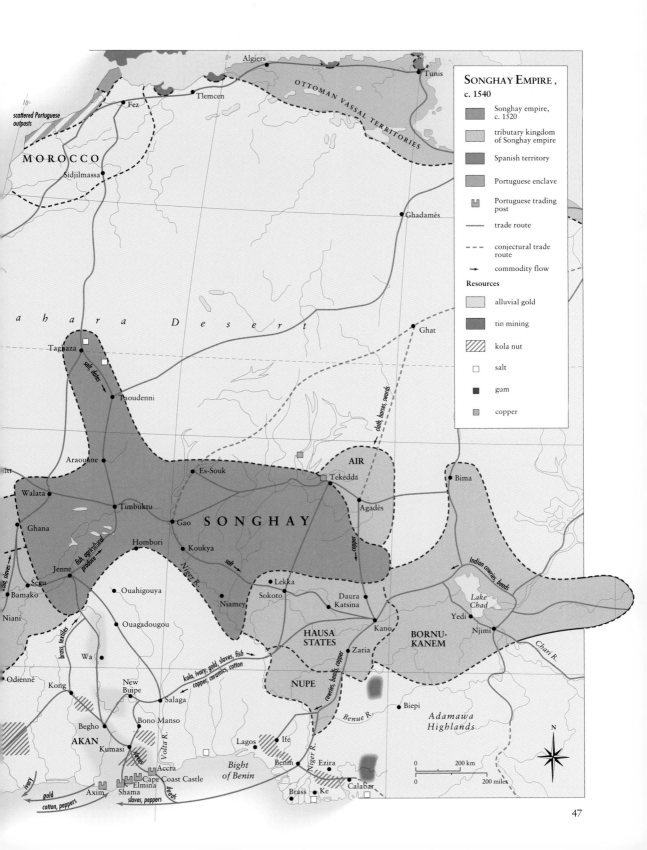

Algiers

Tunis

OTTOMAN VASSAL TERRITORIES

Tlemcen

Fez

10°

scattered Portuguese
outposts

MOROCCO

Sidjilmassa

Ghadamès

S a h a r a   D e s e r t

Ghat

Taghaza

salt, dates

Taoudenni

Araouâne

Es-Souk

AIR

Tekedda

Bima

Walata

Timbuktu

Agadès

Ghana

Gao

SONGHAY

Hombori

Koukya

Jenne

fish, agricultural
produce

Segu

Bamako

Ouahigouya

salt

Lekka

Niamey

Sokoto

Daura
Katsina

Lake
Chad

Yedi

Niani

Ouagadougou

Kano

BORNU-
KANEM

Njimi

Chari R.

Wa

HAUSA
STATES

Zaria

Odienné

Kong

New
Buipe

Salaga

NUPE

Biepi

Adamawa
Highlands

N

Begho

Bono Manso

Volta R.

AKAN

Kumasi

Lagos

Ifé

Benin

Ezira

Accra

Cape Coast Castle

Elmina
Shama

Axim

Bight
of Benin

Brass

Ke

Calabar

Niger R.

Benue R.

Niger R.

cloth, horses, swords

copper

copper

Indian cowries, beads

cowries, beads, copper

kola, ivory, gold, slaves, fish

copper, ceramics, cotton

brass, textiles

slaves

ivory

gold

cotton, peppers

slaves, peppers

beads

cloves

salt →

0   200 km

0   200 miles

SONGHAY EMPIRE,
c. 1540

Songhay empire,
c. 1520

tributary kingdom
of Songhay empire

Spanish territory

Portuguese enclave

Portuguese trading
post

trade route

conjectural trade
route

commodity flow

Resources

alluvial gold

tin mining

kola nut

salt

gum

copper

BENIN AND BORNU-KANEM

BENIN, c. 1500

Benin was a centralized city-state, founded about a thousand years ago, in southern modern-day Nigeria, west of the Niger Delta. Its people were known as the Edo and their rulers as *obas* (kings). King Ewedo was the strongest of the Benin kings, and expanded their empire around 1300. Under his successor, Ewuare, the city of Benin acquired broad streets, secure walls, and a powerful army with which to extend its rule from the Niger Delta to coastal Lagos. By the time the Portuguese arrived on the Benin coast, its empire was advanced in terms of both art and trade. The Edo sold slaves to the Portuguese in exchange for ivory, pepper, and cotton, which they in turn then traded with other societies in the interior.

Idia, mother of Oba Esigic, a ruler of Benin, was granted the right to establish her own places of worship in return for using her mystic powers to bring victory in Benin's war against the Igala people. Brass heads with long beaded caps were cast to decorate the altars.

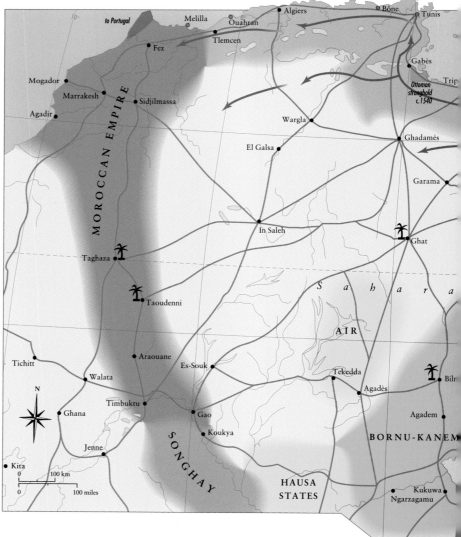

The people who lived around Lake Chad, the Kanuri, established the Bornu-Kanem trading empire, the rulers of which belonged to the Sefawa dynasty, and by the twelfth century were converted to Islam. Mai Dunama Dibalemi's reign (1210–1248) witnessed the strengthening of the Kanem empire, which then controlled the trade routes north of Lake Chad to the cities of the Sahara and the North African coast. The state survived for a hundred years, and by the fourteenth century, Umar, a king of the Sefawa dynasty, had built a new capital at Bornu to replace Njimi, which had been lost to the neighboring Bulala people.

In the fifteenth century, Bornu-Kanem regained its glory in the reign of Idris Alooma (1580–1603), who extended the empire to Murzuk in the north and Darfur in the east, governing through provincial governors and also establishing trade with the Ottoman rulers of Cairo. The empire traded in horses, metalware, salt, and copper from the northern and eastern Saharan states, which they exchanged for kola nuts, gold, and ivory.

Alameen Ben Mohammed el Kanemy, sheikh of Bornu, from an engraving c. 1826.

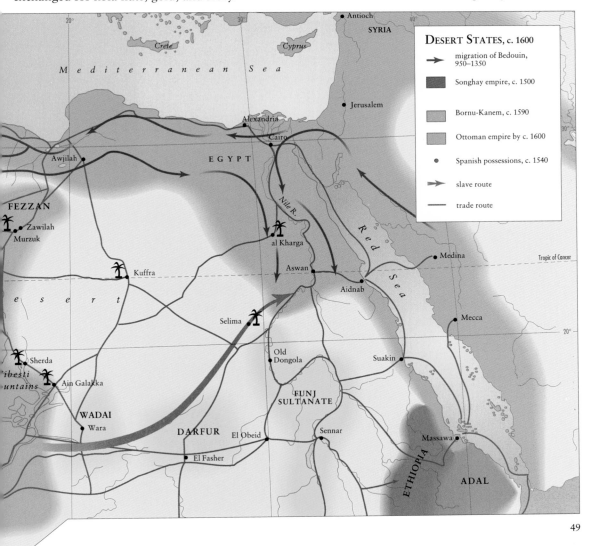

THE HORN OF AFRICA TO C. 1500

The proximity of northeast Africa to key sea and trade routes has resulted in its being influenced by many different peoples and cultures, becoming a complex blend of linguistic, ethnic, and religious groupings.

The Islamic Arab invasion of Egypt in AD 639 brought an end to the Roman and Byzantine empires. By then, the Coptic Church had become the symbol of Egyptian resistance. There was also Coptic resistance to the new Muslim rulers of the Christian South.

Trade already flourished between northeast Africa and Asia, with the Byzantine traders in the area being replaced by Arabs using the Red Sea and Indian Ocean routes. Cushitic-speaking people invaded and occupied the areas along the interior trade routes as well as the coastal towns. The invaders shared a blend of faiths: traditional African religions, Islam, and Christianity.

The Muslim Somalis expanded from the Horn inward and occupied the coastal areas up to the Biuba basin from Zeila to Brava and Mogadishu. By 900 Zeila, south of Djibouti, was the most important Muslim trading center, and came to dominate the life and economy of non-Muslim communities in the interior. First, a sultanate of Shoa was created, then the kingdoms of Ifat and Adal; the Muslims began converting Somalia's predominantly pastoralist inhabitants.

The Christian kingdoms of Nubia, Alodia, Nobatia, and Makuria existed in the Nile Valley until the advent of the Islamic Mameluke empire in 1275 and the establishment of the Islamic Funj sultanate.

The 13th century church of St. George, one of a number of churches at Lalibela carved from solid rock.

In Ethiopia meanwhile, by 1200, the Zagwe kings had seized power from the kings of Axum and were ruling the country from their capital at Adefa in the central highlands, controlling Axum, Amhara, and Shoa. Dahlaks Island was their most important trade outlet connecting to the port of Zeila. Although the kings were Christian, the traders who settled along the routes and in the towns were Muslim. The Zagwe had a large army with which they controlled the land and established Christian settlements as far south as Lake Tana, Gojjam, and Shoa. Most of the conquered regions were ruled by Christian military leaders who set up monasteries, collected taxes, and ensured the protection of traders. However, by fomenting religious conflict against their Christian rulers, the Muslim traders were able to extend their influence from Zeila into the interior, taking control of the eastern and central parts of the kingdom.

The Zagwe kingdom disintegrated and was succeeded by a new dynasty, which claimed descent from King Solomon. The Solomonic kings moved their capital to Shoa, from where they forcefully expanded their Christian empire, slowing the spread of Islam. They invaded the land around the Blue Nile occupied by non-Christian tribes, and displaced the Kalenjin and other pastoralists from the White Nile to the area northwest of Lake Victoria and to the Kenya Highlands. By 1540 the Ethiopians controlled Felasha, Gojjam, and Damot, together with Muslim Dawaro, Hadya, and Bali, and they had again expanded southwest of Lake Tana.

The Later Iron Age, between AD 1000 and 1500, was a period of much ethnic migration in the northeastern interior. Displaced pastoralists arriving from the north in turn triggered the spread of Nilo-Saharan-speaking southern Sudanic and Ethiopic peoples. Western river-lake Nilotes, southern Nilotes, and eastern Nilotes became dispersed in the Great Lakes region. Western Nilotes, mainly Iwo-speaking, may have moved as far south as present-day Nkore, Rwanda, and Burundi to form the Hima and Tutsi inhabitants of the area. Ironworking, herding, and cereal-growing southern Nilotes moved from the northwest of Lake Turkana into the areas east of Lake Victoria. The Nyanza intermingled and absorbed the Cushites of the region, creating the Kalenjin people of Kenya's western highlands and the Dadog of central Tanzania. Eastern Nilotes also from the northwest of Lake Turkana migrated and became the Karamajong and Maasai of northeastern Uganda, and of central Kenya and northern Tanzania respectively. The period is also marked by the formation of chiefdoms like the Chwezi dynasty of Kitara, with its capital at Bigo Bya Mugenyi.

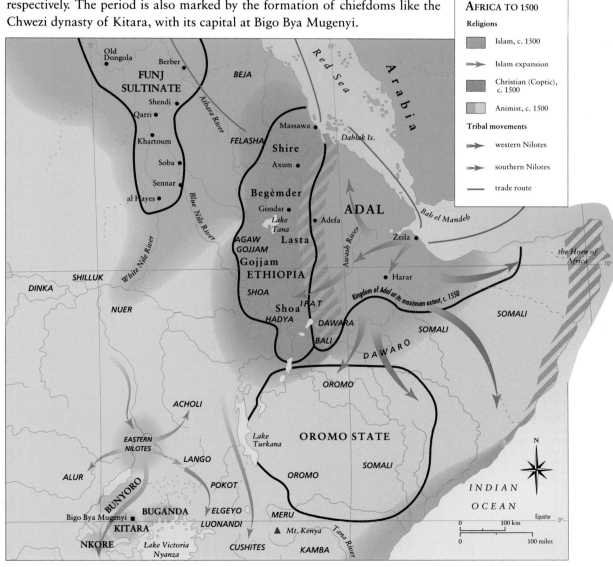

THE HORN OF AFRICA TO 1500

Religions

Islam, c. 1500

Islam expansion

Christian (Coptic), c. 1500

Animist, c. 1500

Tribal movements

western Nilotes

southern Nilotes

trade route

GREAT ZIMBABWE

Great Zimbabwe was inhabited by the ancestors of Africans living in present-day Zimbabwe. Zimbabwe means royal court in Shona. It is these people who, over a thousand years ago, first built the walls of Zimbabwe to encircle the dwellings of their kings. Great Zimbabwe is the largest of the many stone ruins, zimbabwes, in Zimbabwe. The Great Zimbabwe ruins are an example of Africans who over five centuries ago had already developed construction skills. It is an enormous stone wall encircling several enclosures and may have been surrounded by smaller stone walls and mud huts. Nearby is the hill where once there were stone bird figures belonging to the chief's oracle. Zimbabwes were occupied by men of importance belonging to the ruling elite. Probably built in medieval times, around AD 1300, the walls can be compared with the great pyramids of Egypt or the castles in Ethiopia, evidence of the develoment of technological skills in the empire-states and kingdoms in Africa. These men were skilled metalworkers and also builders in stone and brick. For a long time Great Zimbabwe remained a cult center for the Shona.

Toward the end of the nineteenth century European adventurers plundered the ruins, looting golden ornaments from the graves. Contrary to some European myths that Great Zimbabwe was not the work of Africans, expert investigators such as David Randall-MacIver and Gertrude Caton-Thompson have concluded that the ruins were constructed by Africans who developed their own traditional arts and skills.

The fortification wall of Great Zimbabwe. The structures seen today date from the Rowzi hegemony, c. 1500, though the site had been important for several hundred years.

The building of these stone structures began around AD 1100 and was carried out by the Shona, ancestors of the present-day Shona-speaking people of Zimbabwe. One of the greatest kings of the period was Mutota, king of the Karanga, who, having moved the capital from the Great Zimbabwe ruins, created a kingdom that stretched from the Zambezi to the Limpopo River. His military conquests earned him the title, "Mwana-Mutapha," meaning "king of plundered lands." When his son, Matope, succeeded him the kingdom was expanded to reach Mozambique and the East African coast. Great Zimbabwe's prosperity depended on its connections with the East African coastal Swahili towns, especially Kilwa. Local people mined gold and copper which they exported and in exchange imported manufactured goods, cotton, porcelain, and beads. Matope failed to hold the huge empire together and when he died in 1480, the empire split into two, the Mwanamutapa lands of the north ruled by Tongwa, and the Rowzi kingdom in the south ruled by Changamira.

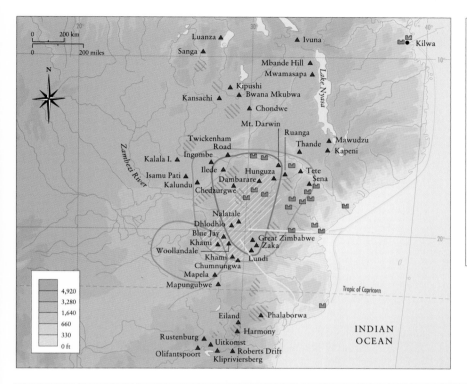

GREAT ZIMBABWE

▲ Iron Age site

⌂ Portuguese fort

⌂ Islamic fort

▨ copper mining and working area

▨ gold mining and working area

→ major route of the gold trade

⬭ area under control of the Shona monarchy based at Great Zimbabwe

⬭ Mwanamutapa territory after 1480

⬭ Torwa territory after 1480

Luanza
Ivuna
Kilwa
Sanga
Mbande Hill
Mwamasapa
Lake Nyasa
Kipushi
Kansachi
Bwana Mkubwa
Chondwe
Mt. Darwin
Ruanga
Twickenham Road
Thande
Mawudzu
Kalala I.
Ingombe
Kapeni
Zambezi River
Ilede
Hunguza
Tete
Isamu Pati
Dambarare
Sena
Kalundu
Chedzurgwe
Nalatale
Dhlodhlo
Blue Jay
Khami
Great Zimbabwe
Woollandale
Zaka
Khami
Lundi
Chumnungwa
Mapela
Mapungubwe
Tropic of Capricorn
Eiland
Phalaborwa
Harmony
Rustenburg
Uitkomst
INDIAN OCEAN
Olifantspoort
Roberts Drift
Kliptiviersberg

4,920
3,280
1,640
660
330
0 ft

0   200 km
0   200 miles

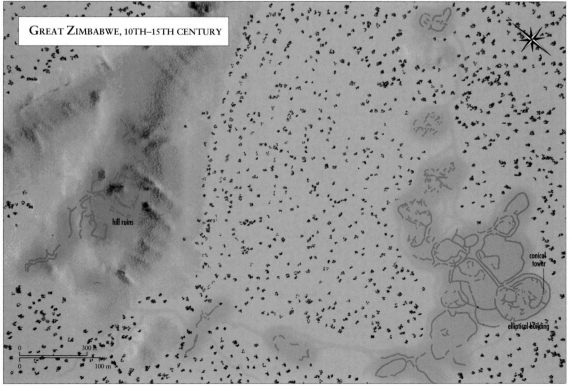

GREAT ZIMBABWE, 10TH–15TH CENTURY

hill ruins

conical tower

elliptical building

0   300 ft
0   100 m

THE SPREAD OF ISLAM

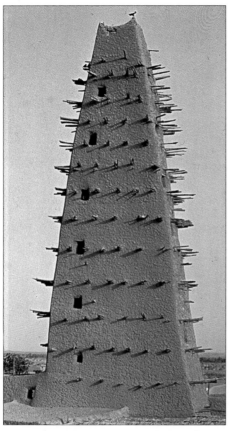

Originally built in the 14th century, the mosque at Agades is made of mud; its structure is constantly renewed by workers bearing new mud up the wooden posts that protrude from the sides and serve as scaffolding.

A 16th century Islamic pillar tomb at Kunduchi on the East African coast, embedded with late Ming plates.

The founder of the Islamic religion, the Prophet Mohammed, was born in Mecca in AD 570, and in 622 he fled on a Hijra with his followers to Medina, where he started a distinctive community that observed no difference between civil and religious laws. He appointed caliphs (deputies), who played both a political and a religious role in their communities. The religion experienced three major periods: 622–800 was a time of conquest, settlement, and amassing of power and wealth; 850–1250, the Great Age of Islam, was the period of advance in Europe and Asia, and of Arabic science, architecture, and art; 1250 onward saw the rise of Islam's militarism and the decline of its civilization.

The Islamization and Arabization of Africa first took place in the north in the seventh century. Before its coming, people along the Mediterranean coastline were largely Christian; those in sub-Saharan West Africa and elsewhere had their own traditional beliefs and religions, which usually centered on the worship of nature and the land, and were related to animals like the snake and the ram, which were thought to have supernatural powers. These ancient religions continued even after the introduction of Islam, which was spread by the Berbers (the Sijilmasa and Almoravids) from the north via the trans-Saharan trade routes.

Egypt became predominantly Muslim after the Arab conquest of 639, although it was not until around three centuries later that Islam almost completely obliterated Christianity. From Egypt, Islam spread to northern Sudan and became the religion of the Funj Sultanate. In non-Nilotic Sudan, Islam was introduced by the Mande and Hausa traders.

Islam was established in Northern Libya and Tunisia by Uqba ibn Nafi in 670. The invasion and settlement of northwest Africa by Bedouin tribes in the eleventh century completed and confirmed the spread of Islam in the Maghrib.

From around 650, Islam started spreading along the East African coast to Zanzibar (*Zanj-Bar, Zenj*=Arabic for black) and its islands, and around 695, Arab traders began to introduce it inland along the caravan routes, with Sena near the Zambezi becoming a major center. Muslim settlements and towns like Sofala, a source of gold and iron, and Kilwa, a port used by the gold traders, were established among the local Bantu inhabitants.

Here, though, it was Swahili (a language combining Arabic, Portuguese, and Bantu), and not Arabic itself, that was the lasting imprint of the Arabization of East Africa. The dynasty of the Daybuli (900–1200) marked the first

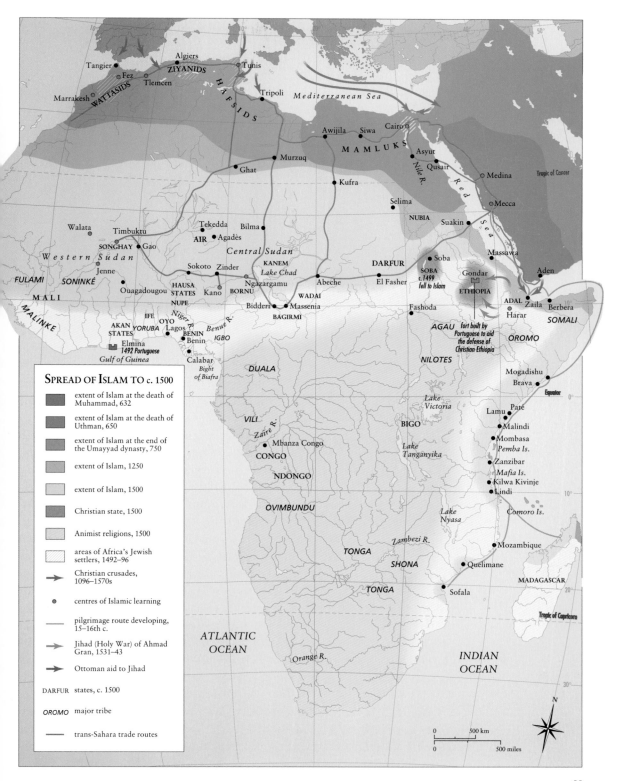

SPREAD OF ISLAM TO c. 1500

- extent of Islam at the death of Muhammad, 632
- extent of Islam at the death of Uthman, 650
- extent of Islam at the end of the Umayyad dynasty, 750
- extent of Islam, 1250
- extent of Islam, 1500
- Christian state, 1500
- Animist religions, 1500
- areas of Africa's Jewish settlers, 1492–96
- → Christian crusades, 1096–1570s
- • centres of Islamic learning
- — pilgrimage route developing, 15–16th c.
- → Jihad (Holy War) of Ahmad Gran, 1531–43
- → Ottoman aid to Jihad

DARFUR   states, c. 1500

OROMO   major tribe

— trans-Sahara trade routes

PLAN OF THE GREAT MOSQUE AT KILWA

```
0                        15 m
0                        50 ft
```

The interior of the Great Mosque at Kairouan in Tunisia, one of the oldest and most important in North Africa. The original foundation dates from 670 AD.

period of full Islamization. At the height of the Great Age of Islam, further waves of Muslim visitors, looking for sources of gold, ivory, slaves, and other merchandise, established permanent settlements along the East African coast. Islam became established on the islands of Zanzibar and Pemba and in settlements along the Banadir coast, which quickly grew into towns. By 1100, stone mosques were built, and the towns were becoming city-states like Kilwa-Kisangani, Malindi, Pate, and Lamu. The intermingling of religions—traditional African beliefs and Islam—was similar to that among the Mandinka, Songhay, and Berbers. The second period, the Shirazi dynasty, which lasted from about 1200 to the end of the thirteenth century, belonged to the Swahili descendants of the Shirazi of Persia, and saw the commercial dominance of Kilwa and Kisimani. Even after the decline of Shirazi, Kilwa controlled the Mafia islands and the ports of the Mozambique coast.

Traders south of the Sahara found it convenient to convert, to maintain good relations with the Berbers; and besides, Islamic theology incorporated appealing precepts of just government and sound economic management. The trade empires of western Africa, like those of Songhay, Mali, and Bornu-Kanem as elsewhere, came to embody combinations of traditional and Islamic beliefs. Rulers like Mansa Musa established centers of Islamic scholarship, which in turn became parts of the network of civilization in northern Africa, in the Maghrib and in the Sahel region (the Sudanic belt). Muslim scholars traveled widely across Africa. Ibn Batutta (1304–1377) was a Moroccan who traveled to Somalia, Kenya, and Tanzania in eastern and northeastern Africa, and across the Sahara to Mali.

RESISTANCE TO ISLAM

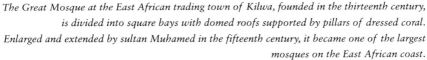

*The Great Mosque at the East African trading town of Kilwa, founded in the thirteenth century,
is divided into square bays with domed roofs supported by pillars of dressed coral.
Enlarged and extended by sultan Muhamed in the fifteenth century, it became one of the largest
mosques on the East African coast.*

In time, in the Sudanic states, Islam began to conflict with the African beliefs that for several centuries had continued to exist alongside it. Since Islam teaches its believers that it is their duty to convert, if need be by force, the region was plunged into jihads (holy wars). Moreover, nominally Muslim states did not always follow the codes laid down by the Koran, and Muslim clerics often saw it as their duty to cleanse their societies, clashing with nominal or non-Muslims. From around 1725, Tuareg, Hausa, and Fulani, together with some Songhay and Mande, waged jihads to overthrow non-Islamic governments. The most important jihad, in Hausaland, was led by Usman dan Fodio (1754–1802), a Fulani. He conquered all the Hausa states, forming an empire with capitals at Sokoto and Gwandu. The jihads spread to the Bornu empire, where his lieutenants established the Hadeja and Katagum emirates, and to the non-Muslim states of Nupe and Oyo, and later Macina. Apart from establishing strong empires, the Fulani jihads further spread Islam to Bauchi and Adamawa in northern modern-day Nigeria. The jihads also led to an increase in the trans-Saharan slave trade, for non-Muslim Africans were routinely captured and sold.

In the 1840s, the eastern African Islamic civilization was extended inland by Ahmed bin Ibrahim to the powerful kingdom of Buganda (now in central modern-day Uganda), where the Arab traders operated with the kabaka's (king's) permission.

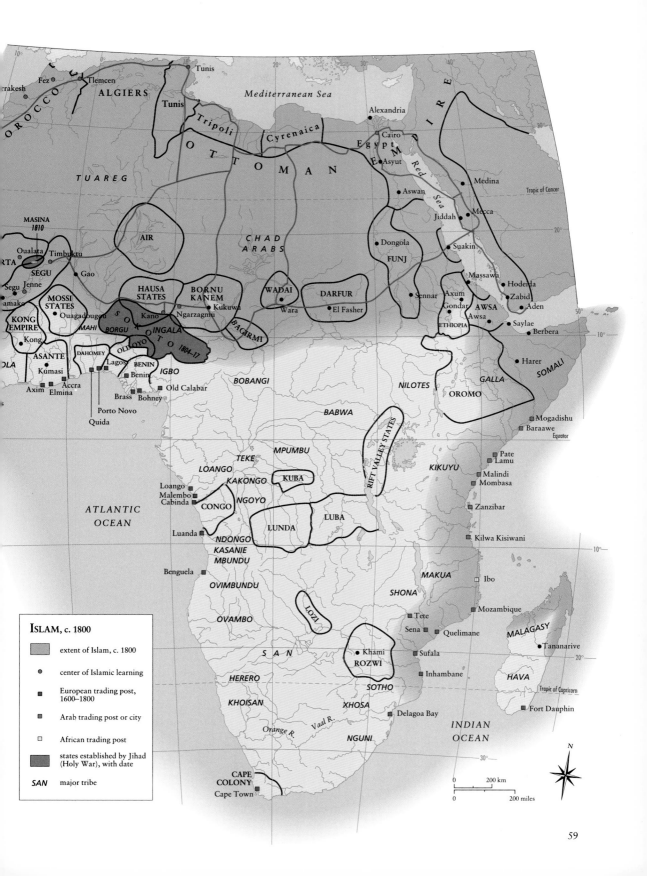

ISLAM, c. 1800

- extent of Islam, c. 1800
- center of Islamic learning
- European trading post, 1600–1800
- Arab trading post or city
- African trading post
- states established by Jihad (Holy War), with date

SAN   major tribe

THE PEOPLING OF MADAGASCAR

Madagascar is separated from Africa by the Mozambique Channel. The island was settled by three different kinds of people: the Wazimba, a Bantu ethnic group from southern Africa; Indonesians who began migrating in the fourth century AD; and Arabs in the eighth century. The majority of the Malagasy population is Malay-Polynesian, and the dominant language, Malagasy, derives from this ethnic mix, and is spoken by a cross-section of groupings and clans. The oldest recorded evidence of the island's peopling are tenth-century Arabic accounts such as Bowork ibn Chamriyar's *Book of Indian Marvels,* which describes the settling of the East African coast by the Waqwaq, who were probably of mixed proto-Malagasy and negroid origin. Using the *waka,* a simple, maneuverable six-crewed canoe with outriggers, the Waqwaq set off from southern India. They traveled over 3,500 miles across the Indian Ocean, first landing on the East African coast, from where they may have been forcibly expelled, and eventually settling on Madagascar. The Indonesians who followed the Waqwaq had larger, faster boats called *kunlun bo.* In the Middle Ages several other peoples migrated to the island, including Arabs, Anatolians, Iranians, and sailors from the Comoros Islands. Apart from the Wazimba, other Africans on the island were imported as slaves by the French.

The earliest European contacts with Madagascar between the sixteenth and eighteenth centuries were limited to occasional landings of Portuguese, French, and Dutch sailors along the southern coast. Pedralves Cabral was the first Portuguese sailor to visit the island, which the Portuguese went on to occupy from 1613 to 1619, turning it into a trading post. In the eighteenth century, Arabs, Portuguese, Dutch, and British all took slaves from Madagascar to Île de France, Cape Colony, the Caribbean, and North America. Sometimes slaves were bought in one part of the island and sold in another, with females often purchased as concubines.

The people of Madagascar are as varied as its five climatic zones. Merinas of the Hauts Plateaux resemble Indonesians, while the Sakalava cattle farmers on the west coast are negroid in appearance, and the Antaifsay and Amaimoro in the east are Malay-Polynesian, also with Arab influences. Under King Andriandahifotsy, the Sakalava had the most powerful early dynasty, establishing the kingdoms of Menabe and Boina. The Merina dynasty was founded by Andriamanelo's successor, Ralambo (1575–1610), and became powerful during the reign of Andrianampoinimerina (1787–1810). Through diplomacy and conquest he created a large Merina kingdom uniting Ambohimanga, Ambohidratrimo, and Antananarivo. On his death, Radama I ruled until 1828, and was in turn succeeded, in 1861, by the despotic queen Ranavalona I. Armed with British guns, Radama I conquered various small tribes; brought Tamatave, Foulpointe, and Maroantsetra under Merina control; and attacked the Betsimisaraka in 1817 and 1823, the Sakalava in 1822, and the Boina in 1824. European religions and technology became widespread in the eighteenth century, and French penetration reached its peak in the nineteenth.

Across the Indian Ocean came exotic crops with the Malayo-Indonesian migrants. The same paddy field system is used in Madagascar to grow rice as in the ancestral homeland of southeast Asia.

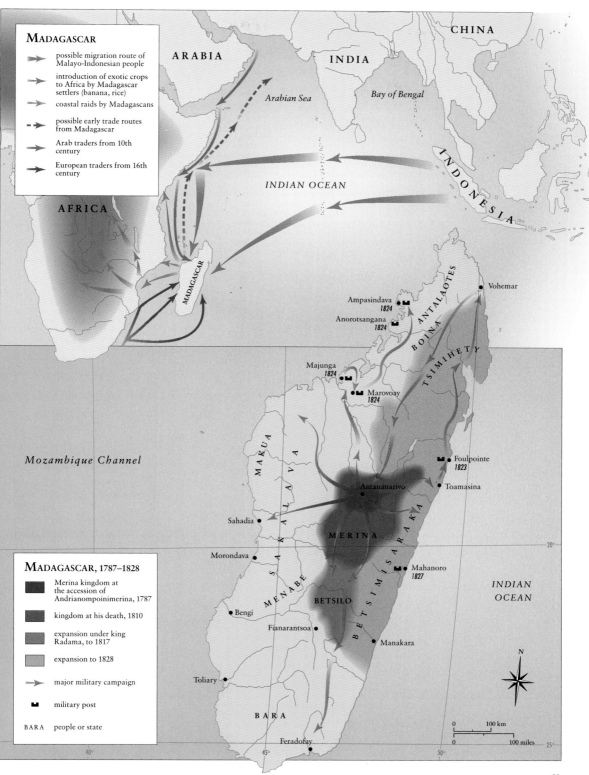

MADAGASCAR

→ possible migration route of Malayo-Indonesian people

→ introduction of exotic crops to Africa by Madagascar settlers (banana, rice)

→ coastal raids by Madagascans

⇢ possible early trade routes from Madagascar

→ Arab traders from 10th century

→ European traders from 16th century

CHINA

ARABIA

INDIA

Arabian Sea

Bay of Bengal

INDONESIA

INDIAN OCEAN

AFRICA

MADAGASCAR

Mozambique Channel

Vohemar

Ampasindava
1824

Anorotsangana
1824

ANTALAOTES

BOINA

TSIMIHETY

Majunga
1824

Marovoay
1824

MAKUA

SAKALAVA

Foulpointe
1823

Antananarivo

Toamasina

Sahadia

MERINA

BETSIMISARAKA

Morondava

20°

Mahanoro
1827

INDIAN
OCEAN

MENABE

BETSILO

Bengi

Fianarantsoa

Manakara

MADAGASCAR, 1787–1828

■ Merina kingdom at the accession of Andrianompoinimerina, 1787

■ kingdom at his death, 1810

■ expansion under king Radama, to 1817

■ expansion to 1828

→ major military campaign

⌂ military post

BARA people or state

Toliary

BARA

Feradofay

N

0   100 km
0   100 miles

40°   45°   50°   25°

61

PART III: EUROPE IN AFRICA

On the eve of European colonization, parallel changes were taking place in Africa. The early nineteenth century witnessed the development of Egypt by Muhammad Ali (1805–1849) into the most powerful North African state, whose prosperity depended partly on the trade in slaves and ivory from Sudan, and partly on foreign investment and finance. Egypt possessed a strong army, mostly staffed by European officers who also administered its provinces. In northeastern Africa, Ethiopia, Sudan, and Somalia experienced political and military struggles, caused mainly by Ethiopia's expansionism, but which also involved Egypt and the earliest intervention of the European powers. Galla raids and Egyptian military might were major obstacles to Ethiopia's ambitions. The unification of Ethiopia, begun by Chief Kassa of Qwara, who declared himself Emperor Tewodros (Theodore), was completed in 1889 by Menelik of Shoa, who acquired weapons from the Europeans in exchange for ivory, and extended the empire to Oromo, Sidama, and Somalia. Menelik defeated the Italians at Adowa in 1896, and Ethiopia remained the only state in Africa to successesfully defeat the European colonial invaders.

In East Africa the eighteenth and early nineteenth centuries saw the migration and establishment in the Great Lakes region of Bantu kingdoms, of which Buganda became the most powerful, despite the strong reign of Kabarega in Bunyoro. The political conflicts in northern Africa affected Buganda and Bunyoro as Egypt tried to bring them under the control of its equatorial province. Meanwhile Kenya was invaded by the Galla, forced south by the expanding Ethiopian empire. At the same time, the activities of the slave traders intensified; at around 1840 the last wave of the Nguni invasions took place around Lake Tanganyika.

Arab merchants such as Tippu Tip and Abu Said established trading empires in central Africa dealing in slaves, ivory, and gold; and, together with the Lunda, Yao, and Nyamwezi, they operated a transcontinental network. On the coast, after the earlier Omani Arab and Portuguese conquest, the period 1740–1840 witnessed a struggle for eastern African trade between Arab clans, the Busaidi Sultans of Oman, and the Mazruis. In central Africa, Congo came under the control of King Manicongo, who in later years had to rely on Portuguese cooperation to keep armed raiders away from his empire. At the same time, in southern Africa, the Bantu-speaking communities of Nguni and Sotho also began the process of state formation.

Southern Africa thus experienced the simultaneous arrival and movement inland of the Dutch settlers and the spread of the Nguni. The expansion of the Zulus was initially led by Shaka and, afterward, Dingane, while the Boers fought the Xhosa for control beyond the Great Fish River. These local conflicts led to British investment in and colonization of large parts of southern Africa.

Christian fundamentalism and commercial opportunism together drove the Europeans into Africa. Portuguese interest was further inspired by a desire to avenge the earlier Muslim conquests of Iberia. They wanted to take over the trans-Saharan gold trade from the Arab middlemen and to gain access to India,

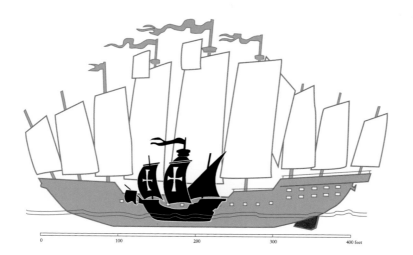

Europeans were not the only visitors to African shores. Around 1415–1417 the Chinese emperor dispatched Admiral Zheng He on a voyage of exploration and diplomacy. Zheng He, at the head of a fleet of huge ships, made contact with the trading towns of the East African coast and gifts were exchanged. The Portuguese arrived some sixty years later, and though exotic, proved a little unimpressive to those who had witnessed or had heard of the earlier Chinese visit.

and in the process destroyed several fine Arab coastal cities. Wherever the Portuguese landed they built fortified trading posts, and on the western coast these led to the decline of the trans-Saharan caravan routes. When Brazil was discovered in 1500, the Portuguese established plantations, marking the beginning of the slave trade in which they were later joined by the Dutch, French, British, Spanish, and Germans. In the sixteenth and seventeenth centuries the Portuguese also introduced Christianity to parts of Africa such as Benin, Congo, and southwest Africa. Egypt too played an active role in the trans-Saharan slave trade to the Middle East and to Europe, and by 1825 Egyptian commanders were raiding Sudanic parts of Darfur, Nuer, Dinka, Gondokoro, and their neighbors for slaves and ivory.

Increasing European interest in Africa in the early nineteenth century led to its exploration, and from 1884, to its partition. Wealthy travelers, part of the humanitarian movement that stopped the slave trade, aimed to navigate the rivers with steamships that would open up remote areas to commerce, European civilization, and Christianity. European adventurers braved dangerous, mosquito-infested regions to find the sources of the great rivers—the Niger, the Nile, the Congo, and the Zambezi. The nineteenth century also witnessed a decline of the old empires of the forest region, especially the Yoruba of Oyo. In their place developed four principal Yoruba states—Fgba, Ijaye, Ibadan, and Igbo—whose wars of rivalry along the coast and inland, enabled the British to establish themselves in what is now Ghana and Nigeria.

The scramble for Africa that began with the Berlin Conference of 1884, ended in 1914 with the continent's complete partition. Britain, France, Germany, and Portugal each wanted to counter the thrust of the others in their areas of influence. British and German agents were very interested in the Lake Victoria region because of its access to the Nile River, and Leopold II of Belgium also sought to extend his Congo Free State to the river. The German and British representatives, Karl Peters and Frederick Jackson, wanted control over trading rights in Buganda, and their claims and counterclaims were only resolved by the Anglo-German treaty of 1890.

This partition of the continent, and the Europeans' missionary activities, laid the foundations of many contemporary political conflicts. Having successfully thwarted the Egyptian advance and resisted Arab domination, Kabaka (King) Mutesa I, for example, continued his attempts to maintain Buganda's sovereignty by inviting both the British Church Missionary Society and the French White Fathers. The three religions of Islam, Protestanism, and Roman Catholicism vied for converts among the young pages in the palace, and Mwanga, Mutesa's successor, became a victim of their rivalries. In the "Christian Revolution" that followed, the British sided with the Protestant party, and in 1893 they declared Uganda a Protectorate.

In 1880 the Europeans' occupation of Africa was largely confined to its coastal regions, but by 1901 they controlled most of the continent. Partition stripped Africans of independence, freedom, and civil rights, and often subjected them to harsh European rule. European racism, rooted in the "scientific" principles of the period, dictated that white people had a duty to govern and civilize Africans, whom they saw as children, but bloody wars of pacification frequently destroyed whole communities, like the Ashanti of Ghana.

Africa would also inherit the European powers' ignorance of traditional African national boundaries; nearly all colonial borders separated friendly ethnic groups and amalgamated hostile ones.

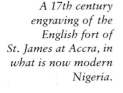

A 17th century engraving of the English fort of St. James at Accra, in what is now modern Nigeria.

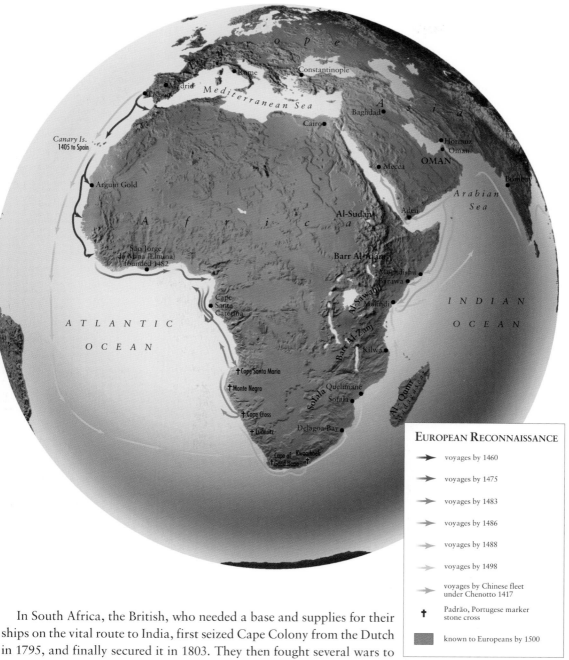

Canary Is.
1405 to Spain

Arguin Gold

Rome
Madrid
Lisbon
Mediterranean Sea

Constantinople

Baghdad

Cairo

Hormuz
Oman
OMAN

Mecca

Bombay

Aden

Al-Sudan

Arabian Sea

Barr Al-Ajam

Mogadishu
Barawa

São Jorge
da Mina (Elmina)
founded 1482

Cape
Santa
Caterina

Al-Sawahil
Malindi

Barr Al-Zanj

Kilwa

ATLANTIC

OCEAN

INDIAN

OCEAN

†Cape Santa Maria

Quelimane

†Monte Negro

Sofala
Sofala

Al-Qumr
Madagascar

†Cape Cross

†Lüderitz

Delagoa Bay

Cape of
Good Hope   Kwaaihoek

EUROPEAN RECONNAISSANCE

→ voyages by 1460

→ voyages by 1475

→ voyages by 1483

→ voyages by 1486

→ voyages by 1488

→ voyages by 1498

→ voyages by Chinese fleet
under Chenotto 1417

† Padrão, Portugese marker
stone cross

☐ known to Europeans by 1500

In South Africa, the British, who needed a base and supplies for their ships on the vital route to India, first seized Cape Colony from the Dutch in 1795, and finally secured it in 1803. They then fought several wars to establish a firm hold on the territories, where gold and diamonds were discovered. Boer Christians believed in the enslavement of black people, and were prompted to move into the interior by the changes brought about by British rule. The Boers' "Great Trek" northward started around 1836 and ended with their foundation of the Republic of Natal, the Orange Free State, and the Transvaal.

PORTUGUESE COLONIZATION

A detail from a world map drawn in 1500 by Juan de la Cosa, showing the African continent.

"We made peace with them, and all over the country the news spread that Christians had come to Cantor. People flocked from all directions, from Timbuktu in the north and from Serra Geley in the south. People also came from Quioquia, a large city surrounded by walls of baked bricks."
Diogo Gomes, Portuguese explorer, 1457

In the fifteenth century, after the plague known as the Black Death, Europe began a period of recovery and expansion. The Portuguese possessing advanced shipbuilding skills had already made contact with northern Africa, and in 1415 they captured Ceuta. The Portuguese king, Henry the Navigator, then masterminded the navigation and conquest of Africa. The Portuguese interest in Africa was motivated by religious zeal and by a desire to avenge the Muslim conquest of Spain and Portugal. In western Africa, the anti-Muslim aim was to convert the Africans to Christianity and turn them to fight Islam by hijacking the lucrative trans-Saharan gold trade from its Arab middlemen.

The Portuguese took Moderate in 1418, and the Azores in 1439. Four years later Diniz Dias and Nuno Trista conquered Arguin in upper Guinea, turning it into a fortified trading base. Diniz Dias then penetrated the coast of Guinea (1444–1445) and captured slaves whom he took back to Portugal as proof of his conquest. In 1469 Fernando Gommes obtained a five-year monopoly of trade along the Guinea coast and of land within a 400-mile radius of his base, and King John II directed Diogo d'Zazmbja to build the castle of São Jorge da Mina (Elmina) to protect and control the gold trade. Other forts were built at Axim, Shama, and Accra.

In 1472 Portuguese sailors reached the Bight of Benin in the Gulf of Guinea, and direct trade exchange—in gold, ivory, spices, manufactured goods, and copper—ensued between the two countries, peaking in the reign of Oba Esigie (1504–1554), who spoke fluent Portuguese. Bases were built on the islands of São Tome and Fernando Po (1453), from where trade with the interior (mainland Congo) was conducted, and sugar plantations were also established on the islands. At this point the Portuguese started to engage in the slave trade, transporting slaves to the islands to work on the plantations, and then to Brazil and to Portugal itself. After Diago Cao's expedition of 1483 to the Congo estuary and Angola, diplomatic relations were established with the king of Congo, Mani Nzinga, and permanent bases built in Angola at Benguala and St. Paul de Luanda. This colony was almost exclusively controlled and settled by slave traders and lasted for nearly a century.

After Vasco da Gama sailed around the Cape, in 1507 the Portuguese established another stronghold in Mozambique Island, from where they traded in gold with the rulers of the Mwanamutapa empire. The Portuguese had learned about Mwanamutapa from the explorer Antonio Fernandes, and later built forts at Sena and Tete on the Zambezi (1572), and at Quelimane on the coast, from which to pursue further inland trade and conquest. They took Swahili towns like Sofala and Inhambane by force, and for their unmolested occupation paid an annual levy to Mwanamutapa. In turn the Portuguese raised taxes from their inhabitants, using slaves to police their property and protect their trade. However, the subsequent rise of the Rozwi destabilized this situation. The Portuguese also established strong links with Kalonga Mzura, the ruler of Malawi, who gave them military support against the Shona. They in turn gave him military support against his neighbors, the Lundu.

On the arrival of the Portuguese in East Africa, the coastal people dismissed them and their boats as puny compared with the Chinese sailing ships that had preceded them. The Sultan of Kilwa sent emissaries and a donation of a giraffe to the Chinese emperor in 1415, and in 1417 the emperor sent a large fleet to Malindi, commanded by Admiral Zeng He. Although no direct trade went on between the two leaders, diplomatic relations were established. In comparison, the Portuguese looted Mombasa and Kilwa in 1505, Brava in 1506, and other cities many times over. The coastal towns agreed to pay the Portuguese tribute, but this pillaging damaged the Indian Ocean trade, bringing decline to a formerly thriving region and shifting trade routes away from the coast. Although the Portuguese established firm control, some cities continued to revolt with support from Turkish warlords. After the revolts of 1585 and 1588, the Portuguese built Fort Jesus at Mombasa in 1592 to protect their East African interests, while farther north they helped Christian Ethiopia in its struggle against Islam.

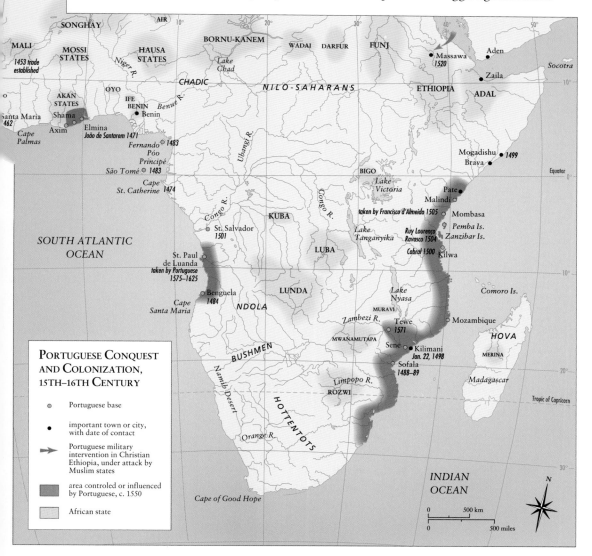

PORTUGUESE CONQUEST AND COLONIZATION, 15TH–16TH CENTURY

- ◎ Portuguese base
- ● important town or city, with date of contact
- → Portuguese military intervention in Christian Ethiopia, under attack by Muslim states
- area controled or influenced by Portuguese, c. 1550
- African state

ARRIVAL OF EUROPEAN TRADERS

An Ashanti gold head, probably a throne or furniture ornament, thought to represent the head of an important enemy killed in battle.

Early European interest and adventure in Africa was motivated by trade and Christian fundamentalism. In West Africa the Mandinka, who inhabited the lands south of the Gambia, traded with the Portuguese from the second half of the fifteenth century. After the Portuguese captured Ceuta in 1415, they began establishing fortified harbors and forts along the West African coast, the largest being Elmina Castle (1482). They bought gold and cottons for resale in Europe; in 1487 set up a trading post in Benin for cloth, beads, and pepper; and by 1501 had established another at Sofala to control the gold trade from Mwanamutapa. In Mwanamutapa they were allowed to establish further trading posts, and in some cases, even to own land. Their ventures in Angola, however, were motivated solely by the slave trade. Along the East African coast too, the

GOLD COAST TRADING FORTS

1 Assinie	18 Anomabu
2 Beyin	19 Egya
3 Ankobra	20 Kormantin
4 Axim	21 Amoku
5 Princestown	22 Tantum
6 Takrama	23 Apam
7 Akwida	24 Winneba
8 Dixcove	25 Beraku
9 Butre	26 Shido
10 Takoradi	27 Accra
11 Sekondi	28 Christiansborg
12 Shama	29 Kpomkpo
13 Kommenda	30 Teshe
14 Elmina	31 Prampram
15 Cape Coast	32 Ada
16 Mouri	33 Keta
17 Anashan	34 Whydah

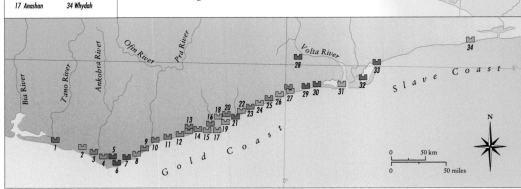

Portuguese built forts, the largest of which was Fort Jesus at Mombasa (1592).

The Dutch were the first northern Europeans to set up a trading post in Africa, when the Dutch East India Company seized all of the Portuguese trading posts along the western coast and set up a supply base at the Cape of Good Hope in South Africa in 1652. In time the Dutch starting moving inland, expanding their market garden trade into farming, and becoming known as Boers (farmers), and later Afrikaners.

As other European companies joined the race to compete for trade with Africa and India, the forts and ports established along the African coast as way stations to India often became launching pads for the penetration of the African interior; examples include Fort Jesus, St. Louis at the mouth of the Senegal, and São Miguel at Luanda. The French arrived in Senegal around 1483 and built St. Louis to dominate the trade along the Senegal and Gambian coasts, while the Portuguese maintained their control of the Gambia River itself. French, Dutch, English, and Portuguese all established themselves along the Slave Coast east of Accra to Lagos, but they did not venture much inland.

Later, the European traders were superseded by concession, or by chartered companies. In East Africa, in the late nineteenth century, the Imperial British East Africa Company acquired a strip of land from the Kenyan coast up to Buganda (Uganda), while the German East Africa Company acquired land in Tanganyika, and the German Witu Company obtained trading rights for Germany in Kenya. Through the South Cameroons Company of 1898 the Germans established their control of Cameroon by acquiring twenty million acres to grow rubber, and followed with a similar land acquisition by the North West Cameroons Company. Likewise, the British South Africa Company, formed by diamond merchant Cecil Rhodes in 1889, occupied Mashonaland and Matabeleland, forming the territory of Rhodesia.

Elmina castle, established in 1482 by the Portuguese, is one of the earliest trading forts on the Gold Coast.

AFRICA, C. 1600

The Maghrib was an important region in both the expansion of Islam and the operation of trans-Saharan trade. The Almohads who took over the Almoravid empire in North Africa and Spain established strict state structures and institutions of learning. The invasion of the Bedouin introduced the Arabic language, which began to displace the indigenous Berber dialects, today spoken only by the Atlas Mountain Berbers in Morocco and the Kabylie Mountain Berbers of Algeria. The Almohads failed, however, to establish a controlled central government or an idea of statehood among the Berber tribes, and started to lose their control in the early thirteenth century.

In the thirteenth and fourteenth centuries, the major empire states were those of the Ziyanids, Hafsids, and Marinids. The Hafsid family controlled Ifriqiya (present-day Tunisia) from about 1129, when it broke away from the disintegrating Almohad empire to become an important agricultural and trading region with profitable trans-Saharan and European trade links, surviving until 1574. The Al-Wahids formed the Abd-al-Wahid empire (present-day Algeria) in 1235. Around 1248, the Marinids established an empire in Morocco that reached its peak during the reign of the Wattasids (1465–1554).

As Christianity reestablished itself in Muslim Spain, the Portuguese and Spanish built strongholds along the Maghrib coast in the fifteenth century. They were too powerful for the Muslim states of Algeria and Tunisia, who had to ally with the Turks to defeat them, thereby extending the Ottoman empire to the region.

The Saadids, a Moroccan nomadic clan led by Saadin, united Morocco and recruited a large army equipped with up-to-date muzzle-loading guns. The Saadid successfully resisted both the invasion of western Maghrib by the Ottoman empire and the invasion of the Portuguese in 1578, in which, at the battle of al-Ksa Kebir, the Portuguese king and Saadin were killed. The Moroccans drove the Portuguese from their Atlantic coast strongholds, and Saadin's successor, Ahmad al-Mansur (1578–1603), consolidated a powerful kingdom whose Spanish mercenaries made a surprise attack on the Songhay army at Tondibi near Gao in 1591, bringing an end to the Songhay empire.

Traditional Berber decoration focused on personal items, jewelry, and weapons, such as this silver dagger hilt imbedded with semi-precious stones.

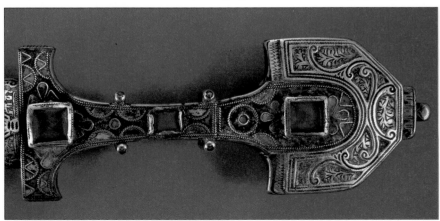

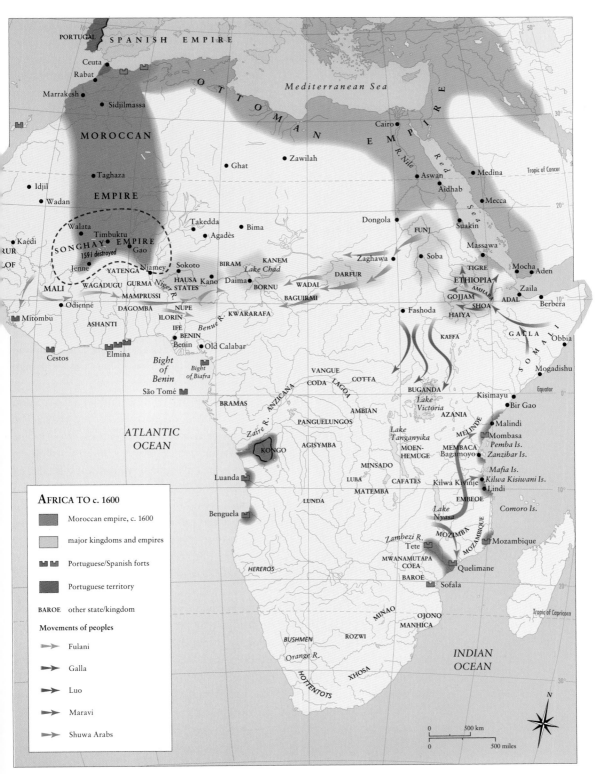

PORTUGAL
SPANISH EMPIRE
Ceuta
Rabat
Marrakesh
Sidjilmassa
Mediterranean Sea

O T T O M A N   E M P I R E

MOROCCAN
Ghat
Zawilah
Cairo
R. Nile
Aswan
Aidhab
Medina
Tropic of Cancer

Taghaza
EMPIRE
Idjil
Wadan

Red Sea

Mecca

Takedda
Bima
Dongola
FUNJ
Suakin
Massawa
Mocha
Aden

Kaédi
Walata
Timbuktu   EMPIRE
SONGHAY
1591 destroyed   Gao
Jenne
YATENGA   Niamey
MALI
WAGADUGU   GURMA
Odienné
DAGOMBA
MAMPRUSSI
ASHANTI
DAGOMBA
ILORIN
NUPE
IFE
BENIN
Benin

Agadès
Sokoto
BIRAM
Lake Chad
KANEM
Daima
BORNU
HAUSA
STATES   Kano
Niger R.

Zaghawa
Soba
TIGRE
ETHIOPIA
GOJJAM
SHOA
HAIYA
Fashoda
KAFFA

WADAI
BAGUIRMI
DARFUR

Zaila
ADAL
Berbera

GALLA
SOMALI
Obbia

Mogadishu

RUR
OF
Mitombu
Cestos
Elmina
Old Calabar
Bight of Biafra
São Tomé

Benut R.
KWARARAFA

Bight of Benin

BRAMAS
ANZICANA
Zaire R.
CODA
LAGOA
COTTA
VANGUE
AMBIAN
PANGUELUNGOS
AGISYMBA

BUGANDA
Lake Victoria
AZANIA

Kisimayu
Bir Gao
Malindi
MELINDE
Mombasa
Pemba Is.
Zanzibar Is.

Equator

ATLANTIC
OCEAN

KONGO
Luanda

LUBA
MINSADO
CAFATES
MATEMBA
LUNDA

MOEN-
HEMUGE
Lake Tanganyika
MEMBACA
Bagamoyo

Mafia Is.
Kilwa Kisiwani Is.
Lindi

Kilwa Kivinje
EMBEOE
Lake Nyasa

Comoro Is.

Benguela

HEREROS

Zambezi R.
Tete
MWANAMUTAPA
COEA
BAROE
Sofala

MOZIMBA
MOZAMBIQUE
Mozambique
Quelimane

Tropic of Capricorn

MINAO
OJONO
MANHICA
ROZWI
BUSHMEN
Orange R.
XHOSA
HOTTENTOTS

INDIAN
OCEAN

N

AFRICA TO c. 1600

- Moroccan empire, c. 1600
- major kingdoms and empires
- Portuguese/Spanish forts
- Portuguese territory

BAROE   other state/kingdom

Movements of peoples

➤ Fulani
➤ Galla
➤ Luo
➤ Maravi
➤ Shuwa Arabs

0   500 km
0   500 miles

71

BLACK GOLD

For many Africans, the last sight of their homeland may have been from the gateway of Elmina castle to the slave ships, waiting nearby.

The Bantu, and other people in eastern, central, and southern Africa, have always enslaved their captives in war. This domestic slavery, however, is not comparable to the international slavery conducted by the Arabs and later by the Europeans. In AD 120 a Greek merchant in Periplus on the Erythraen Sea wrote about the trade in slaves on the East African coast, describing how they were exploited to build pyramids and canals, or as domestic servants. Slaves were exported to Egypt and other Mediterranean countries at the height of the Meroë kingdom and during the period of the Roman occupation. Later, Arab settlements on the East African coast were centers of trade in slaves and ivory to Arabia, Persia, and the East. As early as the seventh century AD, slaves were being exported to southern Iraq and China from Zanj (Arabic for "black") to work as soldiers, household servants, and farm laborers.

In West Africa, the Portuguese first brought slaves from Benin and the Niger Delta both for the Portuguese home market, and for sale locally in the Gold Coast. This trade then started to boom with the development of sugar plantations in Brazil and the West Indies, for unlike the inhabitants of these newly-colonized lands, Africans were accustomed to hard agricultural work.By 1530 the transatlantic slave trade was thriving and in 1600 Arguin to Sherbro and from Axim to Calabar were its major sources. By the mid-seventeenth century exports of slaves exceeded those of gold, and in the late seventeenth and eighteenth centuries it reached its peak. The Ekpe of the Cross River towns in eastern modern-day Nigeria profited most from the trade, whose merchants bought slaves from the Ibo and transported them in canoes to the coast. Altogether, Portuguese, Spanish, Dutch, French, and British participated in the shipment of more than forty million Africans across the Atlantic.

The transatlantic Middle Passage was an experience not only of violence, brutality, and death, but also of bravery and resistance, for the captives rioted against their enslavers. A terrible so-called triangular trade developed: manufactured goods, especially guns, from Europe to Africa; slaves from Africa for work on the plantations of America, Brazil, and the West Indies; and sugar, rum, and tobacco produced by the plantations back from the Caribbean and the Americas to Europe.

In 1710 the French East India Company conquered the Indian Ocean Islands of Île de France and Bourbon (Mauritius and Réunion), from where they exported slaves to the French colonies in India, French and Spanish West Indies, and Java. Others remained to work on sugar plantations in Mauritius. Slaves were also transported along the Saharan trade routes to Egypt and finally to the Mediterranean countries and Europe, and vice versa; European kings and traders sold white slaves to North Africa and Asia. Under Turkish rule, Egypt actively participated in the capture and sale of slaves from central Sudan, and by the second half of the eighteenth century Arab traders were raiding the East African interior for slaves and ivory with their African partners the Nyamwezi, Bisa, Yao, and Lamba. In Malawi the Bemba, Bisa, and Yao terrorized, captured, and sold their weaker neighbors, and by 1825 Egyptian commanders were raiding Sudanic parts of Darfur, Nuer, Dinka, and Gondokoro, again for slaves and ivory. Slave caravans crisscrossed central and eastern Africa to the coastal towns of Kilwa and Zanzibar, and as Portuguese rule of the coast declined, the Arabs once more took it over.

The slave trade depopulated large areas, like Ndongo in Angola and slowed the economic development of the whole regions of the African continent.

Slavery was officially abolished in the British empire in 1833, the United States in 1863, the League of Nations in 1926, and Saudi Arabia in 1963, but it still lingers on illegally.

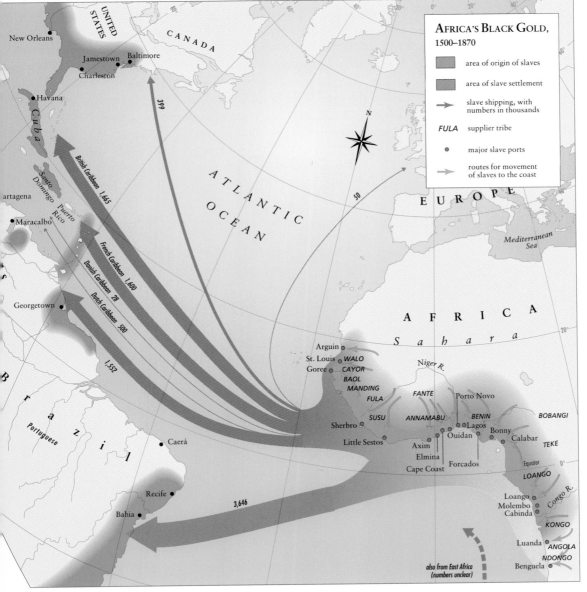

WEST AFRICA, 1800–1875

A combination of factors—international trade, religion, and the Islamic jihads (holy wars)—combined to change the face of West Africa at the beginning of the nineteenth century. The thriving transatlantic and trans-Saharan trade was closely linked with the spreading of Islam. Revolutionary leaders like the skillful, Arabic-educated preacher Usman dan Fodio (c. 1754), asserted that Islam was the only religion by which man should be ruled. The West African jihads of this period began in Futa Jalon (modern Guinea), where in 1725, Fulbe settlers invoked Islam to wage a war against the native pagan farmers who were oppressing them. This uprising sparked off other rebellions in Futa Toro (1776) and in the Hausa states. As a result of these jihads, the Sokoto empire developed under the leadership of Usman to become the most influential state in West Africa. When Yunfa, the King of Gobir, attempted to assassinate Usman, Usman withdrew from the country and in 1804 organized an invasion in which Yunfa was defeated. The success of this jihad led to the invasion of other Hausa states, and by 1808 the whole region was under the control of Muslim rulers. Islam unified the previously divided states, and trade flourished once again. Similar uprisings occurred in Bornu, where the Sefawa dynasty survived only because Muhammad al-Kanemi and his son

The stone palace, or Aban, built c. 1822 by Osei Bonsu at his capital at Kumasi, was intended to impress visitors to his state. He ordered the doorposts and pillars in ivory, the window casings and many other details in solid gold.

Umar, who succeeded in 1835, totally destroyed the old regime. The second West African jihad of the nineteenth century, led by reforming Fulani Muslims, occurred west of Hausaland in Masina, which later became part of the Tukolor empire.

Another empire to rise in the nineteenth century was Mandinka, led by Samori Toure (b. 1830). Samori came from a trading family whose fortunes were always protected by a small but well-trained army, which he modernized and used against the neighboring states. During this period, old empires of the forest region disintegrated, like the Yoruba of Oyo, in whose place developed the four new Yoruba states of Ijaye, Ibadan, Egba, and Igbo. Their wars of mutual rivalry enabled the British to intervene and establish themselves in Yorubaland.

The nineteenth century witnessed a change of pattern in West Africa's external trade; the trans-Saharan camel caravans dwindled, partly because of the changing political landscapes and partly as a result of the increased transatlantic trade, while the latter diversified from slaves to other commodities like vegetable oils. There was also a remarkable change in the type of products sold across the Sahara. Gold and ivory declined, but the demand for slaves in North Africa and the Middle Eastern countries continued.

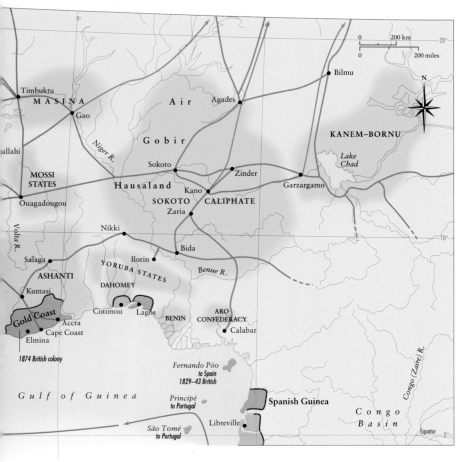

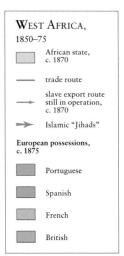

WEST AFRICA,
1850–75

African state, c. 1870

trade route

slave export route still in operation, c. 1870

Islamic "Jihads"

European possessions, c. 1875

Portuguese

Spanish

French

British

KINGDOMS OF CENTRAL AND EAST AFRICA

Mohammed bin Sayed, popularly known as Tippu Tip, after an eye affliction that made him blink continually. He was reputed to be one of the greatest slave dealers in eastern Africa.

At the beginning of the nineteenth century eastern and central Africa were marked with the presence of a mixture of strong centralized kingdoms and smaller chiefdoms. South of the Zambezi River, the Rowzi kingdom developed while other powerful kingdoms evolved in the north. The Rowzi ("the destroyer"), led by Changamira, broke away from the Monamotapa kingdom before the beginning of the nineteenth century to form a confederation of small states referred to as the Rowzi kingdom. By c. 1800, it became the most powerful kingdom south of the Zambezi. The kingdom had a centralized political system. The king kept the Portuguese away from his territory and survived until 1834. Ruins of extensive stone buildings at Khami, Dhlo-dhlo, and Nalatali are evidence of their outstanding building traditions. North of the Zambezi, in present-day Zambia, existed several kingdoms, including the Lunda kingdom of Kazembe, an offspring of the greater Luba kingdom of Mwata Yamvo ("Lord of the Viper"), and the Bemba. Others were the kingdoms of Kaniok, Kalundwe, Kikonja, and Kazembe of Lualaba. The Luba empire was founded on the mineral wealth of copper, iron, and salt deposits. Its territory covered the areas around Kasai and Lulua rivers extending to Lake Tanganyika, an area rich in ivory and copper. The Luba were distinguished by their skills in sculpture and music. Like the Lunda, the Luba empire's decline was attributed to the growing strength of the Nyamwezi and coastal Swahili traders in the nineteenth century. The Lunda, a breakaway group from the Luba kingdom, was located in Luapula Valley. Its monarch continued to be called Mwata Yamvo. Dependent on agriculture, rich salt and copper deposits, and trade links with Swahili and African traders to the east and with Portuguese in Angola and Mozambique, the Lunda became a wealthy and powerful kingdom. An emissary of Mwata Yamvo who moved into the Shaba (Katanga) province to explore the trade in copper and salt set up his own kingdom and took the title Mwata Kazembe. He was the greatest of these kings, and he ruled the land through chiefs. He traded in copper, ivory, salt, and slaves, selling them to Portuguese traders at Tete. The Kazembe kingdom survived until the incursion of Belgian as well as Swahili and Nyamwezi traders toward the end of the nineteenth century. The Bemba, with a well-organized military force invaded the small chiefdoms around Lake Malawi. Their king, Chitimukulu, administered the country through a network of senior chiefs. The kingdom prospered, exchanging slaves and ivory for guns with the Nyamwezi and Swahili traders of the East African coast. The kingdom survived until it was incorporated into the British Protectorate of Northeastern Rhodesia at the end of the nineteenth century

The Lozi kingdom in western Zambia, first ruled by Queen Mwamba, was formed with the settlement of the Lozi on the flood plains of the Zambezi River. The queen ruled

through senior chiefs. While the country was known as Bulozi to the inhabitants, the first Europeans named it Barotseland. In 1833, the expansion of the Zulu empire plus the white northern migration from the Cape destabilized the kingdom. Until 1865 when, under Chief Lewanika, the Lozi regained control of the kingdom, they were ruled by Chief Sebituane of the Kololo. It was chief Lewanika who, at the end of the nineteenth century, handed the country to the British.

By the beginning of the nineteenth century the most important kingdoms in the Great Lakes region were Ankore (Nkore), Buganda, Bunyoro, Toro, Rwanda, Burundi, and Haya. The rival kingdoms of Buganda and Bunyoro were the most powerful in the region. Buganda, bordering Lake Victoria, took advantage of a stable agricultural base, a strong navy, and a regular army to terrorize its neighbors. The king (Kabaka) relied on a centralized administrative structure of chiefs and clan heads to administer the country. Bunyoro, bordering Lake Albert, reached its peak under King (Omukama) Kabarega, who transformed the military prowess of the kingdom to confront invasions from Buganda in the south and from Sudan in the north. The pastoralist kingdoms of Ankore, Haya, Burundi, and Rwanda, organized along class distinctions, were located southwest of Buganda. In Ankore, the Bahima (Hima) pastoralists controlled the government while the peasant agriculturalists, the Bairu, had no freedom of participation in the political affairs of the kingdom. Burundi and Rwanda had political structures similar to those of Ankore. The Batutsi (Tutsi) pastoralists ruled the peasant agriculturalists, the Hutu.

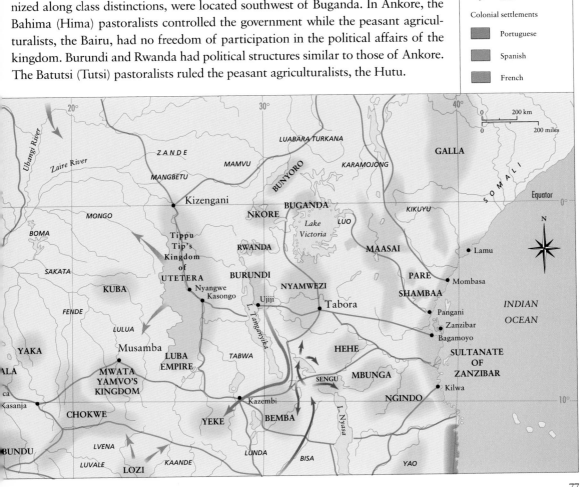

KINGDOMS OF CENTRAL AND EAST AFRICA, c. 1850

African state, 1800–60

trade route

Nyamwezi-Yeke migration

Kololo and Ngomi invaders/settlers

raid

Colonial settlements

Portuguese

Spanish

French

AFRICA, C. 1830

Made during the 19th century, these gold insignia jewelry disks were worn by senior officials at the court of the Ashanti kings.

At the beginning of the nineteenth century the major Muslim states in North Africa—Egypt, Tunis, and Tripoli—were part of the Ottoman empire, and Algiers and Morocco were independent kingdoms. Fezzan, south of Tripoli, was ruled by the pasha of Tripoli, Yusuf Karamanli. He formed trade and diplomatic relations with the central Sudanic states of Bornu and Sokoto, which provided slaves for the market at Tripoli. In 1830, France conquered and occupied Algeria. At this time Egypt was under the leadership of Muhammad Ali (1805–1849), who dominated the region as far as the Red Sea coasts, and had conquered Sudan in 1821, establishing its capital at Khartoum in 1830.

Along the East African coast trade flourished, but it was then disrupted by the Busaidi-Mazrui struggle (1817–1836), and despite the Mazrui's alliance with the British they were defeated by Said Sayyid, who took control of the whole coastline. In the interior, trade was at its height; 1830 marked the rise of the new slave trade in East Africa conducted by Zanzibari Arabs, Swahili Arabs, and Portuguese, while Swahili Arab routes crisscrossed eastern and central Africa with ivory and slave centers at Ujiji, Unyanyembe, and Unyamwezi.

By 1830, the southern and central African landscapes were being rearranged by the Mfecane wars and the Nguni invasions of the Zulus. Population pressures in southern Africa, caused partly by the Boer movements and partly by Shaka's miltaristic reign over the Mtetwa in Natal, triggered off the Mfecane. Fleeing tribes destabilized other settlements as they distanced themselves from Shaka's violent onslaughts. They moved north and east to Mozambique, to the High Veld and to the Drakensberg Mountains. The Ngoni, led by Zwangendaba, plundered the Swazi and Tonga, destroyed the Rozwi dynasty, and settled around Lake Malawi. After terrorizing its Tumbuka inhabitants, they moved to the area south of Lake Tanganyika.

In central West Africa, Fulani jihads continued to spread in the Hausa states. Bello, Usman dan Fodio's son, met with rebellions led by Abdullah and the Hausa scholar Abd al-Salam. The Fulani in Bornu and Sokoto also rebelled, and the Oyo empire that had risen in the late eighteenth century was disintegrating by 1830. The abolition of the Atlantic slave trade not only brought about the creation of two freed-slave colonies, Sierra Leone and Liberia, but also increased British participation in the affairs of the West African states. The Gold Coast became a British possession.

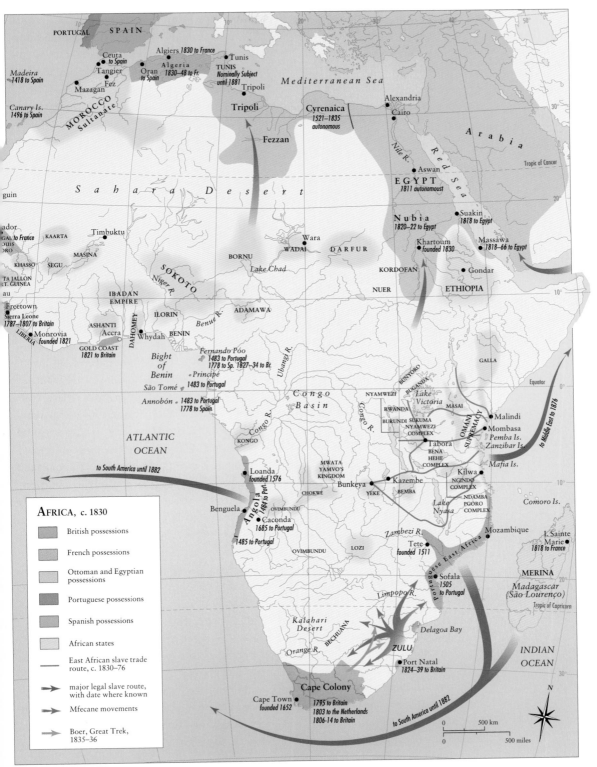

PORTUGAL   SPAIN

Madeira
1418 to Spain

Ceuta
to Spain
Tangier   Algiers 1830 to France   • Tunis
Fez   Algeria   TUNIS
Oran   1830–48 to Fr.   Nominally Subject
Mazagan   to Spain   until 1881   Tripoli

Canary Is.
1496 to Spain

MOROCCO
Sultanate

Tripoli   Cyrenaica
1521–1835
autonomous

Mediterranean Sea

Alexandria
Cairo

A r a b i a

Fezzan

Tropic of Cancer

S a h a r a   D e s e r t   EGYPT
1811 autonoust

Aswan

Nile R.

Red Sea

guin

ador
GAL to France
ouis
ORO

KHASSO   SEGU

KAARTA   Timbuktu

MASINA

BORNU

Wara
WADAI   DARFUR

Nubia
1820–22 to Egypt

Suakin
1818 to Egypt

Massawa
1818–66 to Egypt

TA JALLON
T. GUINEA
au

SOKOTO   Lake Chad

Niger R.

Khartoum
founded 1830

KORDOFAN   Gondar

Freetown
Sierra Leone
1787–1807 to Britain

IBADAN
EMPIRE

NUER   ETHIOPIA

LIBERIA   Monrovia
founded 1821

ASHANTI   ILORIN
Accra   DAHOMEY

GOLD COAST
1821 to Britain

Benue R.   ADAMAWA

BENIN
Whydah

Bight
of
Benin

Fernando Póo
1483 to Portugal
1778 to Sp. 1827–34 to Br.

Príncipe
1483 to Portugal

São Tomé

Annobón   1483 to Portugal
1778 to Spain

Ubangi R.

GALLA

Equator

Congo
Basin

BUNYORO
BUGANDA
NYAMWEZI
RWANDA   Lake
Victoria
BURUNDI SUKUMA
NYAMWEZI
COMPLEX

MÁSAI

OMANI SUPREMACY

Malindi
Mombasa
Pemba Is.
Zanzibar Is.

to Middle East to 1876

ATLANTIC
OCEAN

Congo R.

KONGO

Congo R.

MWATA
YAMVO'S
KINGDOM

Tabora
BENA
HEHE
COMPLEX

Mafia Is.

Kilwa
NGINDO
COMPLEX

to South America until 1882

Loanda
founded 1576

CHOKWÉ

Bunkeya   Kazembe
YEKE   BEMBA

NDAMBA
PGORO
COMPLEX

Benguela

Angola
1484 to Port.

OVIMBUNDU

Caconda
1685 to Portugal

1485 to Portugal

OVIMBUNDU   LOZI

Lake
Nyasa

Comoro Is.

Zambezi R.   Mozambique

Tete
founded 1511

Portuguese East Africa

L. Sainte
Marie
1818 to France

MERINA

Madagascar
(São Lourenço)

Kalahari
Desert

Orange R.

BECHUANA

Limpopo R.

Sofala
1505
to Portugal

Delagoa Bay

ZULU

Port Natal
1824–39 to Britain

Tropic of Capricorn

INDIAN
OCEAN

N

Cape Town
founded 1652

Cape Colony

1795 to Britain
1803 to the Netherlands
1806–14 to Britain

to South America until 1882

0   500 km

0   500 miles

AFRICA, c. 1830

- British possessions
- French possessions
- Ottoman and Egyptian possessions
- Portuguese possessions
- Spanish possessions
- African states
- East African slave trade route, c. 1830–76
- major legal slave route, with date where known
- Mfecane movements
- Boer, Great Trek, 1835–36

EUROPEAN EXPLORERS, 1840–1889

A fanciful representation of Shoua women, from the kingdom of Bornu, taken from Denham's Journey across the Sahara; *c. 1826.*

Lacerda Almeida pioneered Portuguese expeditions when in 1795 he attempted to cross from Tete on the east coast to Luanda in the west. Almeida died midway through his journey, but nearly thirty years later, Pedro Baptista and Anastasio Jose, both *pombeiros* (slaves who worked for Portuguese traders), succeeded in crossing from Angola to Tete.

However, even by the late eighteenth century very little was known in Europe about the interior of Africa. Interest in the continent increased in the early nineteenth century. Apart from James Bruce, who, between 1768 and 1773, had traveled to Gondar in Ethiopia and Sennar in the Funj empire, in search of the Blue Nile, no significant exploration had been undertaken. The sources of the Niger River in West Africa, Nile River in East Africa, Congo River in central Africa, and Zambezi River in southeastern Africa remained mysteries.

Travelers, members of the humanitarian movement that helped to stop the slave trade, aimed to navigate the rivers and ply them with steamships, which would open up the areas for trade and commerce, European civilization, and Christianity. The African Association (1788) sponsored Mungo Park's initial exploration of the Niger River in 1795, and won government finance for a second expedition of 1805 (Park himself was drowned at Bussa rapids in 1806). Other explorers who traveled under the Association's auspices were Denham and Clapperton, who crossed the Sahara (1823–1825), Lander and his brother, who were the first Europeans to reach the source of the Niger River(1830–1832), and Heinrich Barth, who traversed central and western Sudan (1850–1855).

Most Europeans were deterred by malaria-bearing mosquitoes from adventuring into the West African interior. In central Africa, David Livingstone crossed the land preaching the gospel and advocating an end to slave trade. In 1856, Richard Burton and John Speke, following the Arab trade routes, attempted finally to locate the source of the Nile River. Both reached Lake Tanganyika, and Speke traveled on to Lake Nalubaale, which he named Victoria. The Royal Geographical Society (formerly the African Association) then supported Speke and Grant's 1860 expedition which led them to Buganda, where the king gave them permission to journey on at last to the source of the Nile. They then followed the river northward, on their way meeting Samuel Baker, another Englishman, who was traveling south from Egypt. Baker continued south to Bunyoro, and in 1864 reached Lake Mwitanzige, which he named Albert.

Krapf and Rebman, two German travelers, were the first white men to reach the Kilimanjaro and Kenya mountains (1849), while other Germans—Gerhard Rohlfs, Gustav Nachtigal, and Barth—explored the trade routes of western Sudan and North Africa. In 1874 Nachtigal crossed western Sudan between Lake Chad and the Nile. To match the other European powers, in 1874 France sponsored Pierre Savorgnan de Brazza to travel to the Congo Basin on a political-commercial expedition and learn more about the Congo River. He returned to France in 1878, having explored the Ogowe estuary, and established the presence of a network of streams between Stanley Falls and Stanley Pool, the region later to be called French Gabon.

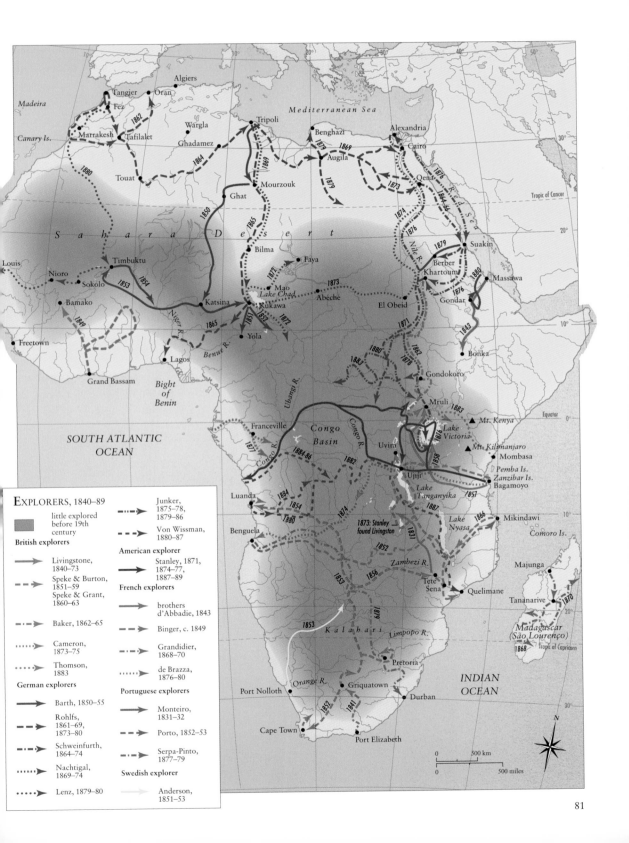

Madeira

Mediterranean Sea

Canary Is.

Algiers
Tangier
Oran
Fez
Marrakesh
Tafilalet
Wargla
Ghadamez
Touat
Ghat
Tripoli
Benghazi
Augila
Alexandria
Cairo
Qena
Mourzouk

Sahara Desert

Tropic of Cancer

Louis
Nioro
Sokolo
Bamako
Freetown
Timbuktu
Bilma
Faya
Berber
Khartoum
Suakin
Massawa
Gondar
Bonka
Katsina
Rukawa
Mao
Lake Chad
Abéché
El Obeid
Niger R.
Benue R.
Yola
Grand Bassam
Lagos
Bight of Benin

SOUTH ATLANTIC OCEAN

Franceville
Congo Basin
Congo R.
Ubangi R.
Uvira
Mruli
Mt. Kenya
Equator
Lake Victoria
Mt. Kilimanjaro
Mombasa
Ujiji
Pemba Is.
Zanzibar Is.
Bagamoyo

Luanda
Benguela
Lake Tanganyika
1873: Stanley found Livingstone
Lake Nyasa
Mikindawi
Comoro Is.
Zambezi R.
Majunga
Tete
Sena
Quelimane

Kalahari
Limpopo R.
Tananarive
Madagascar (São Lourenço)
Tropic of Capricorn

INDIAN OCEAN

Pretoria
Orange R.
Griquatown
Durban
Port Nolloth
Cape Town
Port Elizabeth

EXPLORERS, 1840–89

little explored before 19th century

British explorers

Livingstone, 1840–73

Speke & Burton, 1851–59
Speke & Grant, 1860–63

Baker, 1862–65

Cameron, 1873–75

Thomson, 1883

German explorers

Barth, 1850–55

Rohlfs, 1861–69, 1873–80

Schweinfurth, 1864–74

Nachtigal, 1869–74

Lenz, 1879–80

Junker, 1875–78, 1879–86

Von Wissman, 1880–87

American explorer

Stanley, 1871, 1874–77, 1887–89

French explorers

brothers d'Abbadie, 1843

Binger, c. 1849

Grandidier, 1868–70

de Brazza, 1876–80

Portuguese explorers

Monteiro, 1831–32

Porto, 1852–53

Serpa-Pinto, 1877–79

Swedish explorer

Anderson, 1851–53

0   500 km
0   500 miles

N

PARTITION, 1880–1885

By 1880, apart from the interior of southern Africa most European occupation of Africa was confined to the coastal regions. Naval bases were established along the coasts occupied by France to protect their merchants. In the next twenty years, with exploration and missionary activities adding to the commercial pressures, the European powers scrambled for every inch of the continent, carving it into bits. By 1901, apart from Ethiopia and Liberia (a colony of black emigrants from America), most of Africa was owned by the Europeans.

The partition stole African independence, freedom and civil rights, and subjected the continent to harsh European rule. The scramble for Africa climaxed with a vicious acquisition of land involving bloody conflicts between either European or white-organized African state armies. In West Africa the British, for example, used brutal force against the Ashanti of Ghana. The people of Congo and various states in East Africa, Madagascar, Morocco, Ethiopia, and Sudan shared similar experiences.

Economically, Europe's industrialized countries needed a source of raw materials as well as a market for their manufactured goods. Nationalist public opinion and prestige spurred the European leaders to acquire land in Africa. Racism rooted in the scientific principles of the period imbued white people with a belief that they had a duty to govern and civilize Africans, whom they equated with children. Traders and explorers urged their governments to tap into Africa's vast wealth, while missionaries advocated the religious conversion of the dark, savage continent. Egypt, hitherto in France's sphere of influence,

After the Berlin Conference, these Ashanti women would become subjects of the British empire. Their children may have lived to see independence some seventy years later.

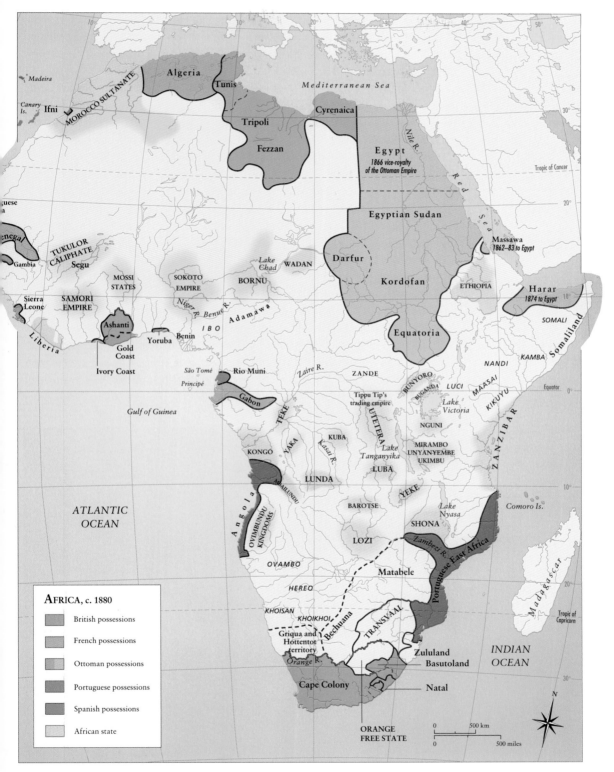

Madeira

Canary
Is.

Ifni

MOROCCO SULTANATE

Algeria

Tunis

Mediterranean Sea

Tripoli

Cyrenaica

Fezzan

Egypt
1866 vice-royalty
of the Ottoman Empire

Nile R.

Red Sea

Tropic of Cancer

Egyptian Sudan

Massawa
1862–83 to Egypt

uese
a

Senegal

TUKULOR
CALIPHATE
Segu

Gambia

Lake
Chad

WADAN

BORNU

Darfur

Kordofan

ETHIOPIA

Harar
1874 to Egypt

MOSSI
STATES

SOKOTO
EMPIRE

Sierra
Leone

SAMORI
EMPIRE

Niger R.

Benue R.

Adamawa

SOMALI

Somaliland

Liberia

Ashanti

Gold
Coast

Yoruba

Benin

IBO

Ivory Coast

São Tomé

Rio Muni

Príncipe

Zaire R.

ZANDE

Equatoria

NANDI

KAMBA

BUNYORO

NGANI

LUCI

MAASAI

KIKUYU

Equator

Gabon

TEKE

Tippu Tip's
trading empire

BUGANDA

Lake
Victoria

Gulf of Guinea

YAKA

KUBA

Kasai R.

UTETERA

Lake
Tanganyika

NGUNI

MIRAMBO
UNYANYEMBE
UKIMBU

ZANZIBAR

KONGO

LUBA

ATLANTIC
OCEAN

MBAILUNDU

LUNDA

YEKE

BAROTSE

Lake
Nyasa

Comoro Is.

Angola

OVIMBUNDU
KINGDOMS

SHONA

Portuguese East Africa

OVAMBO

LOZI

Zambezi R.

Matabele

Madagascar

HEREO

Tropic of
Capricorn

KHOISAN

KHOIKHOI

Bechuana

TRANSVAAL

INDIAN
OCEAN

Griqua and
Hottentot
territory

Orange R.

Zululand

Basutoland

Cape Colony

Natal

ORANGE
FREE STATE

N

AFRICA, c. 1880

British possessions

French possessions

Ottoman possessions

Portuguese possessions

Spanish possessions

African state

0   500 km

0   500 miles

was occupied by Britain in 1882 with Germany's support. In turn Germany helped France to compensate its loss of Egypt with alternative territories in Africa. Bismark then took possession of Togoland, Cameroons, Southwest Africa (Namibia), and Tanganyika.

The Berlin Conference of 1884–1885 was organized so that the powers could divide their spoils by negotiation. It ratified their invasions and drew borders to be observed in all later adventures. From their coastal bases in Senegal, the French occupied Ivory Coast, French Guinea, Dahomey, Gabon, and North Africa west of Libya. From the Gold Coast the British took Ashanti, and from Lagos they took Nigeria, Sierra Leone, and the Gambia. The Portuguese occupied Angola, Mozambique, Guinea-Bissau, and the nearby islands. Italy took Libya, Eritrea, and part of Somalia. King Leopold of Belgium took the Congo Basin. In East Africa, Britain, in order to protect Egypt from French incursion and secure the Nile Valley, occupied Uganda, later acquiring Kenya when the French took Madagascar (in 1885), and Morocco (in 1912). In 1934 Italy took control of the unified state of Libya, formerly Tripolitania, and Cirenaica.

Because European powers were ignorant of the traditional boundaries in Africa, nearly all colonial borders separated common ethnic groups and combined hostile ones. The Nigeria-Cameroon border, for example, split the Emirate of Adamawa; the Ghana-Togo border split the Ewe; and six ethnic groups were split in half by the borders separating Liberia, Sierra Leone, and French Guinea. The same mistakes were repeated throughout Africa, most of whose people were conquered not so much by the Europeans' technological superiority, as by their own disunity.

European officials talk with local chiefs. Photographed in the Congo around 1900.

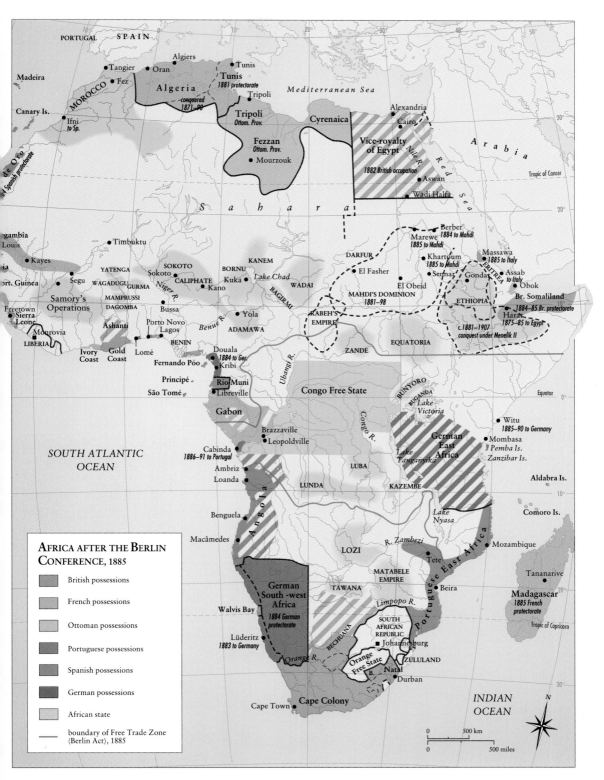

PORTUGAL SPAIN

Madeira

MOROCCO
Canary Is.
Ifni to Sp.

de Oro
and Spanish protectorate

Tangier
Fez
Oran
Algiers
Tunis
Tunis
1881 protectorate

Tripoli

Algeria
conquered 1871–90

Mediterranean Sea

Tripoli
Ottom. Prov.

Cyrenaica

Fezzan
Ottom. Prov.
Mourzouk

S a h a r a

Alexandria
Cairo

Vice-royalty
of Egypt

1882 British occupation

Aswan

Wadi Halfa

Arabia

Red Sea

Tropic of Cancer

egambia
Louis

ia
Kayes

ort. Guinea
Segu

Freetown
Sierra
Leone

Monrovia
LIBERIA

Timbuktu

YATENGA
WAGADUGU
MAMPRUSSI
DAGOMBA

Samory's
Operations

SOKOTO

Sokoto

GURMA

Niger R.

Bussa

Ashanti

Ivory
Coast

Gold
Coast

Lomé

KANEM

BORNU

CALIPHATE
Kano

Kuka

Lake Chad

WADAI

BAGIRMI

Yola

Benué R.

ADAMAWA

Porto Novo
Lagos

BENIN

Douala
1884 to Ger.
Kribi

Fernando Póo

Principé

São Tomé

Rio Muni

Gabon

Libreville

DARFUR

El Fasher

RABEH'S
EMPIRE

ZANDE

Ubangi R.

EQUATORIA

Marewe
1885 to Mahdi

Berber
1884 to Mahdi

Khartoum
1885 to Mahdi
Sennar

El Obeid

MAHDI'S DOMINION
1881–98

Congo Free State

Congo R.

BUNYORO
BUGANDA
Lake
Victoria

Massawa
1885 to Italy

Gondar

Assab
to Italy

Obok

ETHIOPIA

ERITREA

Br. Somaliland
1884–85 Br. protectorate
Harar
1875–85 to Egypt

c.1881–1907
conquest under Menelik II

Witu
1885–90 to Germany

Mombasa
Pemba Is.
Zanzibar Is.

Equator

SOUTH ATLANTIC
OCEAN

Brazzaville
Leopoldville

Cabinda
1886–91 to Portugal

Ambriz
Loanda

Benguela

Macâmedes

Angola

German
East
Africa

Lake
Tanganyika

LUBA

LUNDA

KAZEMBE

Lake
Nyasa

LOZI

R. Zambezi

Tete

MATABELE
EMPIRE

Aldabra Is.

Comoro Is.

Mozambique

Tananarive

Madagascar
1885 French
protectorate

Tropic of Capricorn

AFRICA AFTER THE BERLIN
CONFERENCE, 1885

British possessions

French possessions

Ottoman possessions

Portuguese possessions

Spanish possessions

German possessions

African state

boundary of Free Trade Zone
(Berlin Act), 1885

German
South-west
Africa
1884 German
protectorate

Walvis Bay

Lüderitz
1883 to Germany

Orange R.

TAWANA

BECHUANA

Beira

Portuguese East Africa

Limpopo R.

SOUTH
AFRICAN
REPUBLIC
Johannesburg

Orange
Free State
B.
ZULULAND
Natal
Durban

Cape Town

Cape Colony

INDIAN
OCEAN

N

0   500 km

0   500 miles

CHRISTIANITY IN AFRICA

Kwanmaqwaza mission station in Zululand, a watercolor sketch from c. 1880.

> "I go back to Africa to try to make an open path for commerce and Chritianity."
> *Dr. David Livingstone,* missionary and explorer, 1857

Christianity reached North Africa in AD 189–232. In the Maghrib, although the Romans persecuted the Christians, Donastic Christians continued to practice, while in Egypt, Monophysite Christians formed the Coptic Church, using the Coptic language to replace the Melkite Greek. Between the fourth and seventh centuries AD, Monophysite missionaries took Christianity southward along the Nile Valley to Nubia and Axum (present-day Ethiopia) and its wider spread was only halted by the Islamic conquest of North Africa and Egypt. In Ethiopia there were failed attempts by the Jesuits to convert the Coptic Christians to Catholicism.

In the sixteenth and seventeenth centuries, the Portuguese introduced Christianity to parts of Africa, including Benin, Cape Verde, São Tomé Islands, Congo, and Southwest Africa, although many of these proselytizing missions were rendered unsuccessful by their conflict with the religious and political structures of the countries they visited. With the abolition of the slave trade, there arrived further missionaries who believed that non-Muslim Africans were pagan and superstitious and that the liberated slaves should be converted. They came from Britain, United States, Germany, France, Belgium, and the Netherlands, and worked hand in hand with explorers like Park, Stanley, and Livingstone. Missionary societies such as those of the London Churches, the Anglicans, the Baptists, and the Wesleyan Methodists portioned out territories of operation and went to work.

Along the lower Congo, a Baptist missionary station around 1884 at "Bayneston."

By the time the Christian missionaries reached Buganda (now Uganda) in the

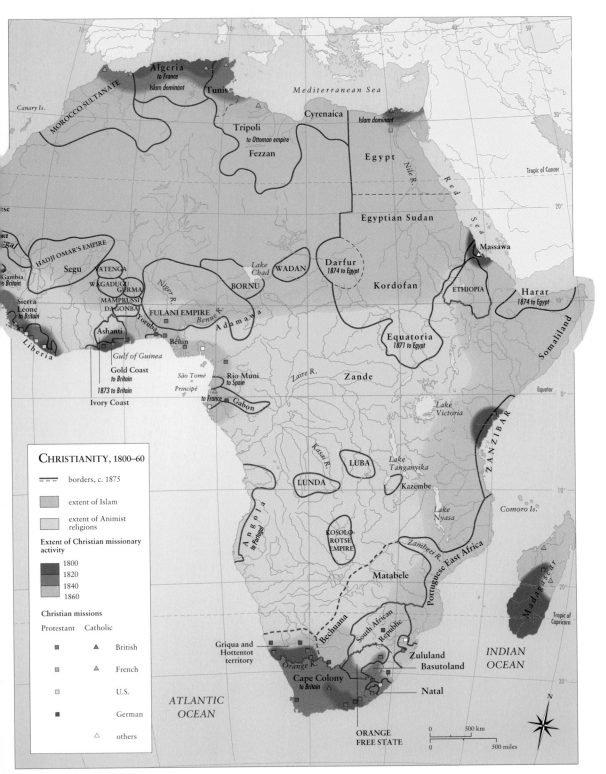

Canary Is.

MOROCCO SULTANATE

Algeria
to France
Islam dominant

Tunis

Tripoli
to Ottoman empire

Fezzan

Cyrenaica

Mediterranean Sea

Islam dominant

Egypt

Nile R.

Red Sea

Tropic of Cancer

20°

Egyptian Sudan

esc

Senegal

HADJI OMAR'S EMPIRE

Segu

YATENGA

WAGADUGU
GURMA

MAMPRUSSI
DAGOMBA

Gambia
to Britain

Sierra
Leone
to Britain

Liberia

Ashanti

Benin

Gulf of Guinea

Gold Coast
to Britain

1873 to Britain

Ivory Coast

São Tomé

Principe

to France

Rio Muni
to Spain

Gabon

Niger R.

Lake
Chad

WADAN

BORNU

FULANI EMPIRE

Benue R.

Adamawa

Yoruba

Massawa

Darfur
1874 to Egypt

Kordofan

ETHIOPIA

Harar
1874 to Egypt

Equatoria
1871 to Egypt

Somaliland

Zande

Zaire R.

Kasai R.

LUBA

LUNDA

Lake
Victoria

Equator

Lake
Tanganyika

Kazembe

ZANZIBAR

Lake
Nyasa

Comoro Is.

CHRISTIANITY, 1800–60

	borders, c. 1875
	extent of Islam
	extent of Animist religions

Extent of Christian missionary activity

1800
1820
1840
1860

Christian missions

Protestant	Catholic	
■	▲	British
■	▲	French
□		U.S.
■		German
	△	others

Angola
to Portugal

KOSOLO-
ROTSE
EMPIRE

Zambezi R.

Portuguese East Africa

Matabele

Bechuana

Griqua and
Hottentot
territory

Orange R.

Cape Colony
to Britain

ORANGE
FREE STATE

South African
Republic

Zululand

Basutoland

Natal

Madagascar

Tropic of
Capricorn

INDIAN
OCEAN

ATLANTIC
OCEAN

0   500 km

0   500 miles

N

late 1870s, Arabs had already built a number of mosques in the country. Missionaries from the British Church Missionary Society arrived in 1876, followed by the London Missionary Society, and the French Catholic White Fathers in 1878, and the Belgian African Association in 1879. Mutesa I, King of Buganda, noted that the differences between the Roman Catholic and Protestant missions were as wide as those between the Muslims and the Christians. His heir, Mwanga, exploited these differences, executed twenty-two young Christian converts (known as the Uganda Martyrs), and sparked off the religious wars. The quelling of the conflict in 1893 ushered in the British Protectorate.

In West Africa, early missionary work by Portuguese and French Roman Catholics faded and was only revived after the French started their colonial expansion, by which time German and American Protestant missions were active in the region too. Religious visitors tended to go to countries where they shared political and commercial interests: American Protestants went to Liberia, while the British, some of whom were Wesleyans, went to Sierra Leone, Nigeria, and the Gold Coast. Missionary work was usually restricted to areas near the coast, and converts to the church were educated to become teachers, clerks, doctors, priests, and administrators. Later, with more colonial expansion, Africans broke away to start their own churches adapted to local forms of worship. In Sierra Leone, the missionaries based at Freetown ministered to the liberated slaves, and their ultimate goal was to establish an independent African church. African converts like Reverend Samuel Crowther, a Yoruba, and first bishop of the Niger Territories (1864), helped spread Christianity throughout the region.

A missionary post at Entebbe in Uganda, c. 1890.

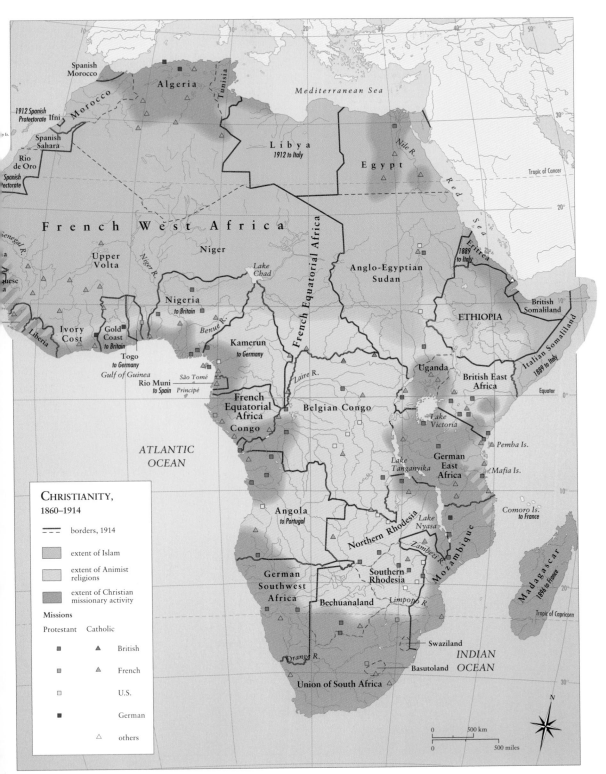

Spanish
Morocco

Algeria

Tunisia

Mediterranean Sea

1912 Spanish
Protectorate Ifni

Morocco

L i b y a
1912 to Italy

E g y p t

Nile R.

Red Sea

Tropic of Cancer

30°

Spanish
Sahara

Rio
de Oro
Spanish
Protectorate

20°

F r e n c h   W e s t   A f r i c a

Senegal R.

Niger

Niger R.

Upper
Volta

Lake
Chad

French Equatorial Africa

Anglo-Egyptian
Sudan

Eritrea
1889
to Italy

British
Somaliland

10°

*guese
a*

Nigeria
to Britain

Benue R.

ETHIOPIA

Liberia

Ivory
Coast

Gold
Coast
to Britain

Kamerun
to Germany

Zaire R.

Uganda

British East
Africa

Italian Somaliland
1889 to Italy

Togo
to Germany
Gulf of Guinea

Rio Muni
to Spain

São Tomé

Príncipe

French
Equatorial
Africa
Congo

Belgian Congo

Lake
Victoria

Equator

0°

ATLANTIC
OCEAN

Pemba Is.

Lake
Tanganyika

German
East
Africa

Mafia Is.

Angola
to Portugal

10°

CHRISTIANITY,
1860–1914

borders, 1914

extent of Islam

extent of Animist
religions

extent of Christian
missionary activity

Missions

Protestant Catholic

■   ▲   British

■   ▲   French

□   △   U.S.

■   German

△   others

Northern Rhodesia

Lake
Nyasa

Zambezi R.

Mozambique

Comoro Is.
to France

Madagascar
1896 to France

German
Southwest
Africa

Southern
Rhodesia

Limpopo R.

Tropic of Capricorn

20°

Bechuanaland

Orange R.

Swaziland

Basutoland

INDIAN
OCEAN

30°

Union of South Africa

N

0   500 km

0   500 miles

CENTRAL AFRICA AND CONGO

Central Africa is divided by the Congo River into the areas between Sudan and southern Africa, Cameroon and Angola, and Mogadishu and Mozambique. Europeans maintained interests along the coastline and in western Congo, but Arab Swahilis from the eastern coast, led by Tippu Tip (1837–1905), controlled most of central Africa.

In September 1880, naturalized French explorer Pierre Savorgnan de Brazza (1852–1905), signed a treaty with the Makoko in the upper Congo, by which King Iloo of the Bateke surrendered his land to the French. Like Stanley, who was signing treaties elsewhere in the Congo Basin on behalf of Belgian King Leopold II (1865–1909), Brazza signed treaties with other local chiefs on behalf of the French. These treaties, often just exchanged for cloth and alcohol, were ratified by the French government in November 1882, and in 1884 to 1885 the French laid claim to a large equatorial region. Brazza's adventures also covered the area around the lower Congo, extending as far as Ubangi Chari. Portugal remained in control of Angola, which she conquered by force of arms, and farther east, Germans occupied Tanganyika in 1885 and to the west, German Cameroon.

In 1884 a conference was convened in Berlin to legitimize King Leopold's personal possession, the central Congo, which he referred to as "The Congo Free State." An ardent student of African exploration, Leopold created the African International Association in 1876, the year he hosted the Geographical Conference of Brussels. Under the pretext of eliminating the slave trade from the region, he set up commercial and scientific centers along a route leading from central Africa to Zanzibar on the eastern coast, and extending later to the western coast. In fact these efforts were inspired by his true ambition, which was to carve out a personal African empire. Congo was a vast, fertile basin area inhabited by scattered ethnic groups. Any uncultivated land was declared the possession of the king, and he either kept it or leased it to trading concerns like the Katanga Company to exploit its mineral resources.

Leopold engaged the explorer Henry Stanley to organize a transportation system from the mouth of the Congo River to Stanleyville (Kisangani), and in 1887 he appointed the disreputable Zanzibar slave

This cartoon reflects on little Belgium digesting its huge colonial possessions in Africa. Drawn by G. Julio in 1905.

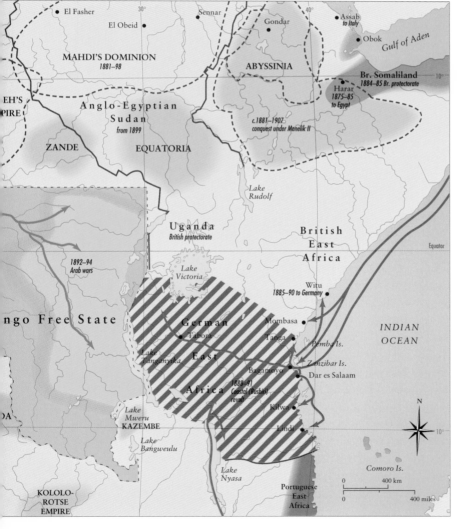

CONQUEST AND
RESISTANCE,
1884–94

British territory

French territory

German territory

Portuguese territory

Spanish territory

Congo Free State

resistance to Belgian rule

British advance

French advance

Belgian advance

trader Tippu Tip, who had wielded power in the area since 1870, to govern a large part of the country. Although Leopold was officially committed to the abolition of the slave trade, his freed slaves were then reemployed in brutal, slavelike conditions, as manual laborers. The shortage of labor forced Leopold to recruit workers from Liberia, Zanzibar, and northeast Africa to work on road and rail construction, and in the army. Authorized by the decree of 1892, African soldiers indiscriminately exacted taxes, which were usually paid in the form of rubber, ivory, or porterage. This meant that in order to pay taxes, people spent much of their time in forests hunting elephants or extracting wild rubber. The system was so abused that in 1908, because of growing local resistance and international pressure, the Belgian government wrested the administration of the colony from King Leopold; it was estimated that since the colony had become his possession, its population had been reduced by about half. Leopold had ruled using a three-tier system combining the church, the crown, and private companies. When the government took over it introduced tight controls and installed a governor-general.

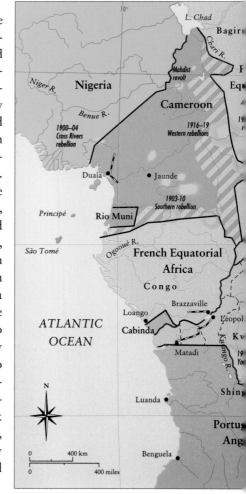

As elsewhere, the Africans were treated by the Belgians with contempt. Only a privileged few received education leading to trade qualifications; fewer still studied for professional courses, which excluded law and medicine; and none were allowed to study in Europe. Most were kept in traditional backwaters, and were subject to travel and drink restrictions. Coordinated, nationwide resistance against the Belgians was difficult, but pressures created during World War II forced people into the towns, and organized action such as union boycotts began. After the Belgian trusteeship of Congo ceased, Rwanda and Burundi achieved independence in 1962. The country was divided into ethnic groups; the Tutsi, favored by the imperialists; and the Hutu who formed the majority of the population. Soon after independence, violence broke out, and the Hutu took control of the government in Rwanda, while in Burundi the Tutsi minority suppressed the Hutu after their failed rebellion of 1972.

A Belgian official holds court in a Congolese village as his African helpers look on. Laws under the Belgian administration could be, and often were, harshly applied to the local people.

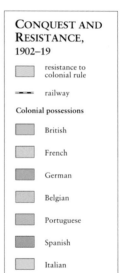

CONQUEST AND RESISTANCE,
1902–19

resistance to colonial rule

railway

Colonial possessions

British

French

German

Belgian

Portuguese

Spanish

Italian

NORTHEAST AFRICA, 1840–1898

Muhammad Ali, 1805–1848, was a modernizing influence on Egypt, making it a considerable power in northeast Africa.

"Those who believed in us as Mahdi, and surrendered, have been delivered; and those who did not were destroyed." Extract from a letter written by *the Mahdi* to General Gordon in Khartoum

The northeast African region at this time was dominated by three main developments: the reunification of Ethiopia, the Egyptian expansion southward, and the Mahdist rebellion. Following the establishment of a new capital in the south, Khartoum, the Egyptians penetrated southern Sudan in search of gold and slaves. Alongside European adventurers like Samuel Baker and George Gordon, European traders were widening their search for slaves. In the 1840s the Egyptians defeated the Shilluk and gained access to a major source of ivory. In order to have effective control over southern Sudan they established forts and garrisons among the Dinka and the Shilluk. Khedive Ismail conquered Darfur in 1874, and employed Baker and Gordon as governors of the so-called Equatorial Region.

In 1881 Muhammad Ahmad from Dongola declared himself the Mahdi ("The Guided One"), and called for a jihad against the nonbelievers. His call attracted the oppressed people in the region, from the Muslim traders to the Kordofan nomads, and in 1885 his men overcame the Egyptians and captured Khartoum. The military strength of the Mahdists persuaded Egyptian forces to abandon their posts on the coasts of the Red Sea and Gulf of Aden. At his death he was succeeded by Khalifa Abdallabi, and the Mahdist state survived until a combined Anglo-Egyptian army destroyed it in 1898, at the battle of Omdurman.

By 1840 the old Ethiopian empire had become divided, and civil war was endemic. Independent states of Bagender, Tigre, and Shoa operated in the Christian highlands, when in 1855, Chief Kassa of Qwara declared himself Emperor Tewodros (Theodore). He laid the foundation of a modern army, which he used to conquer the Galla, and initiated the unification of Tigre and Amhara in the north with Shoa in the south. His mission was brought to an end when the British, led by Robert Napier, overcame his forces in 1868, and he shot himself when Napier raided his fortress at Magdala in 1867. Tewodros was replaced by Kassa, the chief of Tigre, who became Emperor Yohannes (John) IV and fought and defeated the Egyptians at Gundat in 1875 and Gura in 1876. In 1889 Yohannes was in turn succeeded by Menelik of Shoa, who used European weapons, exchanged for ivory, to extend his empire to Oromo, Sidama, and Somalia. In 1896 Menelik defeated the Italians at Adowa. This was the only major victory of African forces over invading Europeans, saving Ethiopia from Italian colonization. Britain meanwhile had occupied the northern Somalia coast (1884–1885), and France had taken Djibouti (1888). To consolidate his borders, Menelik signed treaties with the three imperial powers of Italy, Britain, and France.

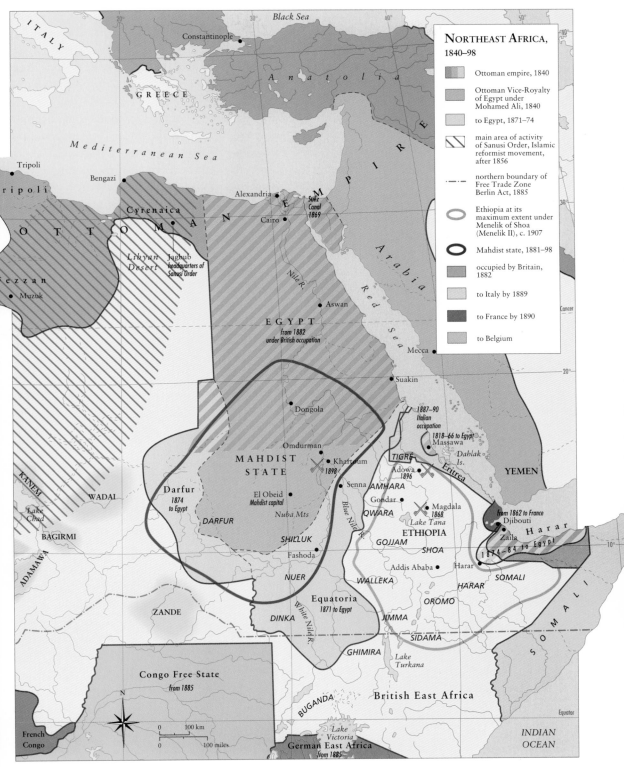

NORTHEAST AFRICA, 1840–98

- Ottoman empire, 1840
- Ottoman Vice-Royalty of Egypt under Mohamed Ali, 1840
- to Egypt, 1871–74
- main area of activity of Sanusi Order, Islamic reformist movement, after 1856
- northern boundary of Free Trade Zone Berlin Act, 1885
- Ethiopia at its maximum extent under Menelik of Shoa (Menelik II), c. 1907
- Mahdist state, 1881–98
- occupied by Britain, 1882
- to Italy by 1889
- to France by 1890
- to Belgium

ITALY

Black Sea

Constantinople

GREECE

Anatolia

OTTOMAN EMPIRE

Mediterranean Sea

Tripoli

Bengazi

Cyrenaica

Alexandria

Suez Canal 1869

Cairo

Arabia

Red Sea

ripoli

OTTOMAN

Libyan Desert

Jaghub headquarters of Sanusi Order

Fezzan

Muzuk

Aswan

EGYPT
from 1882 under British occupation

Mecca

Suakin

KANEM

Lake Chad

BAGIRMI

WADAI

ADAMAWA

Dongola

MAHDIST STATE

Darfur 1874 to Egypt

DARFUR

El Obeid Mahdist capital

Nuba Mts

Omdurman

Khartoum 1898

SHILLUK

Senna

Blue Nile R.

1887–90 Italian occupation

1818–66 to Egypt
Massawa

Dahlak Is.

TIGRE

Adowa 1896

Eritrea

YEMEN

AMHARA

Gondar

QWARA

Lake Tana

Magdala 1868

ETHIOPIA

from 1862 to France
Djibouti

Zaila

Harar

1874–84 to Egypt

GOJJAM

SHOA

Addis Ababa

Harar

SOMALI

NUER

Fashoda

WALLEKA

HARAR

OROMO

SOMALI

ZANDE

DINKA

Equatoria 1871 to Egypt

White Nile R.

JIMMA

SIDAMA

GHIMIRA

Lake Turkana

Congo Free State
from 1885

N

BUGANDA

British East Africa

Equator

French Congo

0   100 km

0   100 miles

Lake Victoria

German East Africa
from 1885

INDIAN OCEAN

CAPE COLONY, 1652–1857

A Danish colonist at his ease, while in the background a black slave is at work, from an 1817 illustration.

In most areas of Africa the Europeans confined themselves to coastal castles and forts. Cape Colony, established by the Dutch East India Company in 1652, was the only exception. Two Khoisan ethnic groupings, named Hottentots and Bushmen by the settlers, had lived in southern Africa since the Stone Age. Others, including the Zulu, Xhosa, and Sotho, had migrated there from around AD 400.

Built on the Cape of Good Hope, Cape Colony was intended to be a supply base for ships sailing on to the Indian Ocean, and Table Bay became the most important port of call for these voyages. Settlers were needed by the Cape both for its defense and to secure adequate supplies of food for the East India seamen. The first Boers (Dutch farmers) arrived in 1657, and numbers increased under the leadership of Simon van der Stel (1679–1700), the son of an Indian woman. These were joined by French religious refugees.

The Khoisan (Hottentots) occupied the land around the Cape of Good Hope and the eastern coastal strip, extending as far as present-day Transkei. As the settlers began to extend inland as migrant farmers, the first Kaffir Wars began. From 1659 onward, the Dutch fought and destroyed Khoisan settlements along the coast, forcing the Africans to become their servants, while inland the freeburger Boers started farming cattle requiring large areas of land. When the Boers expanded eastward toward Zuurveld near the Great Fish River, the Khoisan resisted, first through guerilla wars, and later by moving into the interior ahead of the advancing settlers.

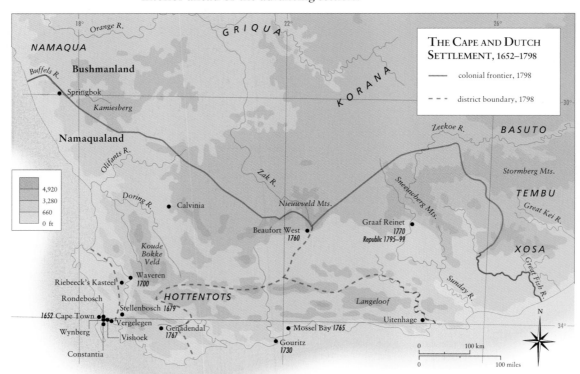

THE CAPE AND DUTCH SETTLEMENT, 1652–1798

——— colonial frontier, 1798

- - - - district boundary, 1798

NAMAQUA

GRIQUA

Orange R.

Buffels R. Bushmanland

Springbok

Kamiesberg

KORANA

Namaqualand

Zeekoe R. BASUTO

Olifants R.

Stormberg Mts.

Zak R.

TEMBU

Doring R.

Calvinia

Nieuwveld Mts.

Sneeuwberg Mts.

Great Kei R.

4,920
3,280
660
0 ft

Beaufort West
1760

Graaf Reinet
1770
Republic 1795–99

XOSA

Koude
Bokke
Veld

Great Fish R.

Waveren
1700

Riebeeck's Kasteel

Sunday R.

Rondebosch

HOTTENTOTS

Langeloof

Stellenbosch 1679

1652 Cape Town

Uitenhage

Vergelegen

Wynberg

Genadendal
1767

Mossel Bay 1765

N

Vishoek

Constantia

Gouritz
1730

0   100 km

0   100 miles

By 1700 the colony had begun importing African, Malay, and Indonesian slaves. Being in the ruling minority, the whites began to distance themselves from the community of Khoisan and slaves. After a brief resistance the Khoisan gave up their land, and settled and intermarried with slaves, and formed a people of mixed race, becoming known as the Cape Colored of South Africa. A branch of the Khoisan called the Korana moved farther inland, raiding the Tswana and their cattle. Another branch called the Griquas, a mixture of pure Khoisan and those of mixed European blood, migrated from the Colony and settled between the Orange and Vaal Rivers.

When Trekboer settlers started moving into the Zuurveld grazing lands of the Xhosa, they sparked off the first Xhosa War of 1779. A magistracy of all districts in southeastern Africa was established at Graaf Reinet in 1786, but in 1795 the settlers rebelled against the magistrate and established the independent Dutch Republic of Graaf Reinet and, later, Swellendam.

The British, wanting to secure the supplies for their ships, first seized Cape Colony from the Dutch in 1795, but the Dutch regained control for a while before finally being ousted in 1803. The British then assembled a colonial army, which they used to defeat the Xhosa of the Zuurveld in the Fourth War of 1811–1812. After the Fifth War in 1818–1819, the British created the first settlement of mixed-race people in the Kat River Valley. When the Xhosa continued their raids, the British fought a Sixth War (1834–1835) after which, under Governor D'Urban, they took control of all Xhosa lands.

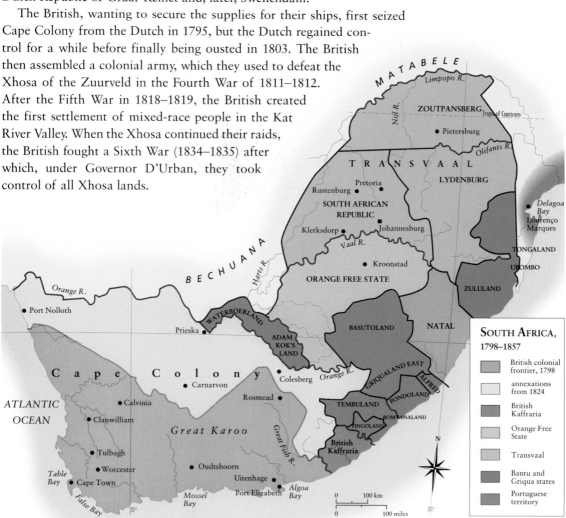

SOUTH AFRICA, 1798–1857

- British colonial frontier, 1798
- annexations from 1824
- British Kaffraria
- Orange Free State
- Transvaal
- Bantu and Griqua states
- Portuguese territory

THE ZULU EXPANSION

Mathlapi's hunting dance, a detail from an illustration by G. F. Angus, 1849.

By the early nineteenth century, the spread of the Bantu southward had led to a concentration of Nguni- and Sotho-speaking Bantu in Southeast Africa. With the arrival of the Europeans in the Southwest, the area became overcrowded. Two upheavals dominate this period, the Mfecani (Nguni for wars and disturbances) and the Great Trek. Three prominent African personalities led strong empires at the time: Sobhuza, chief of the Ngwane (now Swazi) near the Upper Pongola River; Zwide, chief of the Ndwandwe in central Zululand; and Dingisiwayo, chief of the Nguni.

The Zulu of the Nguni clan expanded under the leadership of Dingisiwayo and his successor, Shaka. Shaka was young, powerful, and recklessly brave. He built up a strong army, housed them in official homesteads, revolutionized military structures and tactics, and drilled the army to fight in the "cow horn" formations. His *impis* (regiments) carried *asseggais* (short spears), went through tough physical training, and observed strict discipline. They plundered neighboring tribes, absorbing the young men and women into the Zulu society. In 1818 Shaka defeated the Mthethwa and the Ndwandwe at the Mhlatuse River, and by 1819 he was the most powerful chief in the region.

The expansion of the Zulu forced the neighboring people off their land, in turn destabilizing other communities along their routes of escape. Natal, the Zulu homeland, became surrounded by empty regions abandoned by fleeing people. Zulu leaders like Zwangendaba, Mzilikazi, and Soshangane, who disagreed with Shaka's poilicies, took their regiments off to employ their fighting skills elsewhere. Soshangane defeated Zwangendaba and Maseko in southern Mozambique, and settled his people in Tonga, founding the new kingdom of Gaza. Zwangendaba moved on and settled around Lake Malawi, forming their own chiefdoms. In 1821 Soshangane conquered Mzilikazi and led the Matabele across the Drakensberg Mountains through Sotho, to settle in Botswana.

Other defeated or displaced people moved westward across the Drakensberg Mountains, destabilizing the Tlokwas and Sothos. The Swazi kingdom was a creation of two Zulu refugees, Sobhuza and

Mswazi, and their people. Moshoeshoe built up the Basuto Sotho kingdom from a gathering of refugees, while Sebetwane led the Kilolo Sotho to conquer and settle the Barotse (Lozi) kingdom, the area along the Zambezi previously held by the Tlokwas. Mantatise led yet another group of Sothos westward toward Botswana.

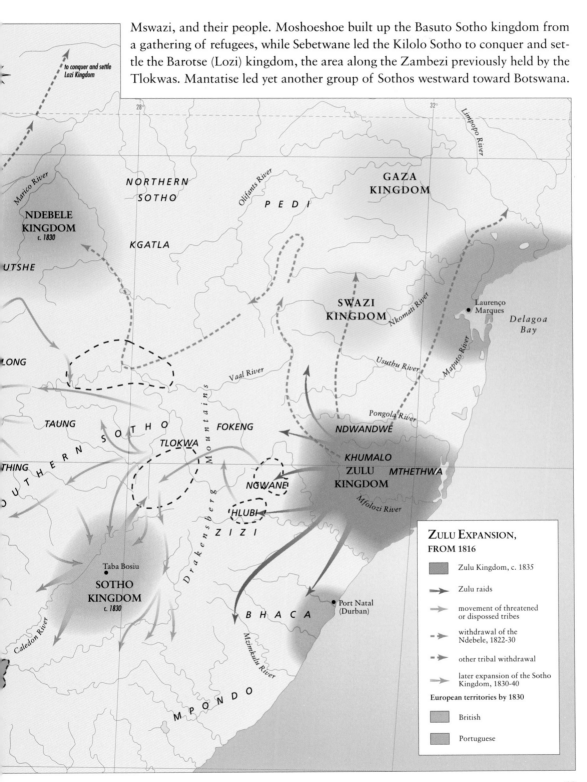

to conquer and settle
Lozi Kingdom

NORTHERN
SOTHO

NDEBELE
KINGDOM
c. 1830

UTSHE

KGATLA

OLIFANTS River

P E D I

GAZA
KINGDOM

Limpopo River

SWAZI
KINGDOM

Nkomati River

Laurenço
Marques

Delagoa
Bay

LONG

Vaal River

Usuthu River

Maputo River

TAUNG

S O T H O

FOKENG

Pongola River

NDWANDWE

THING

TLOKWA

KHUMALO
ZULU   MTHETHWA
KINGDOM

SOUTHERN

NGWANE

Mfolozi River

HLUBI

Z I Z I

Drakensberg Mountains

Taba Bosiu

SOTHO
KINGDOM
c. 1830

Port Natal
(Durban)

B H A C A

Caledon River

Mzimkulu River

M P O N D O

ZULU EXPANSION,
FROM 1816

Zulu Kingdom, c. 1835

Zulu raids

movement of threatened
or disposed tribes

withdrawal of the
Ndebele, 1822-30

other tribal withdrawal

later expansion of the Sotho
Kingdom, 1830-40

European territories by 1830

British

Portuguese

ZULU WARS

After Sir Bartle Frere became governor and high commissioner in South Africa in 1877, he moved swiftly to unify the white states and extend the colony's authority over the neighboring African kingdoms. He passed a law forbidding Africans to own guns, which led to the unsuccessful War of the Guns (1880) against the Basotho. After this failure he moved against the Zulus. The Zulus boasted the most powerful African state, and King Cethswayo, intelligent and popular, ruled through consultation. He reintroduced a strict military regime, even forbidding the men to marry before obtaining the king's permission, usually when they were forty.

Chief among the Zulus' enemies were the Boers of the Transvaal. For Frere, the suppression of the Zulu kingdom therefore offered a solution to all his South African problems. His plan was to have the disputed Blood River Territory handed to Transvaal, in which event the Zulus would go to war and be defeated by the Transvaalers. Transvaal would then favor his plans for federation, and the Zulus would be subjugated. However, Frere's plan backfired when in 1878 the Commission appointed to investigate the dispute decided in favor of the Zulus. Using the excuse of cross-border conflicts around Natal, Frere then demanded that Cethswayo dismantle the Zulus' efficient military organization. Cethswayo responded by assembling his army of 30,000 men.

Zulu soldiers of King Panda's army, from an illustration by G. F. Angus, 1849.

Led by General Thesiger (Lord Chelmsford), about 7,000 British soldiers and 1,000 volunteers attacked the Zulus on three fronts. Cethswayo's *impis* (army regiments) targeted the central column and in a surprise attack on January 22, 1879, at the battle of Isandlwana, they killed 1,600 men. The British troops being marched into Zululand were unprepared and ended up being trapped by Cethswayo. The Zulus employed the traditional military tactics of their ancestor Shaka, and destroyed the advance regiment. Caught off-guard, the troops had no time to organize or even open their boxes of ammunition and were slaughtered. Although the Zulus were finally defeated eight months later at the battle of Ulundi, Frere's plans for a South Africa federation had already been scuppered at Isandlwana. In the end it was defections from Cethswayo's camp, together with British fire power—they introduced machine guns—that helped them win the war. The Zulu kingdom was not occupied, but after Cethswayo was exiled to Cape Town, it was broken into thirteen separate demilitarized areas to which the British appointed the local chiefs.

Prince Dabulamzi ka Mpaande in conversation with trader John Dunn, photographed around 1874. Five years later the prince would lead the Zulu uNdi corps into Natal.

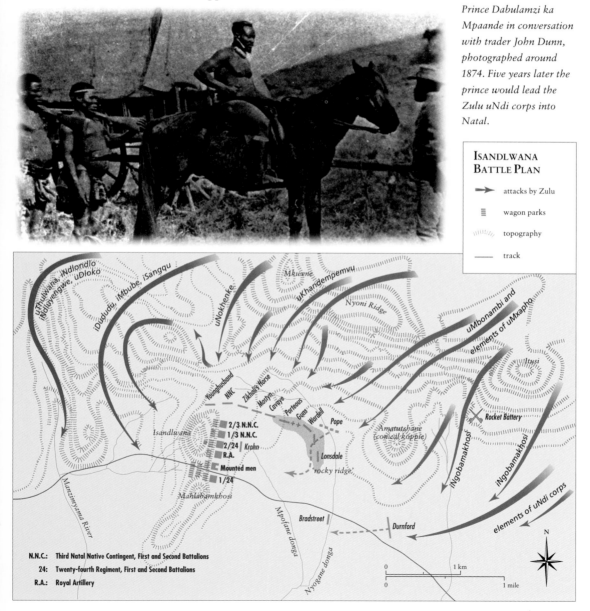

ISANDLWANA BATTLE PLAN

→ attacks by Zulu

▤ wagon parks

⟨⟨⟨⟨ topography

— track

N.N.C.: **Third Natal Native Contingent, First and Second Battalions**
24: **Twenty-fourth Regiment, First and Second Battalions**
R.A.: **Royal Artillery**

THE GREAT TREK, 1836–1846

The trekkers fought many minor and some major battles on their journey north out of the Cape colony. Here a trekker group is wiped out at a place later named Weeping.

The political changes, together with new labor and other philanthropic policies favoring the blacks, prompted the Boers to move northward, away from British control. The practices of the British rulers were in conflict with their version of Christianity, which legitimized the enslavement of black people, or "sons of Ham." The Hottentot Code of 1809 had forced the Khoisan and other black men to carry passes as proof of employment and residence, but the ending of the slave trade prompted missionaries working in Cape Colony to launch a campaign that culminated in the institution of the Ordinance Fifty and the scrapping of the Hottentot Code.

The Great Trek northward started around 1836, by which time the Boer community had evolved into a nation speaking a Dutch dialect, now known as Afrikaans. The trek was a continuation of the movement of settlers inland as well as an opportunistic search for empty land abandoned by indigenous Africans spreading away from their rivals and from the white settlers. The trekkers crossed the Orange River, avoided the Basotho, and congregated near Taba 'Nchu. Some then crossed into the Veld, where they were attacked by Mzilkazi, the Ndebele king. After the Battle of Vegkop in 1836, a few remained to confront him, while others, led by Piet Retief, moved into Natal. The Boers attacked and defeated the Ndebele again in 1837, compelling Mzilkazi to move northward across the Limpopo River. Through force and coercion, Retief negotiated with Dingane, the Zulu king, for land in Natal. Dingane was defeated at the battle of Blood River near Mgungundlovu in 1838, after which he was obliged to negotiate. He was forced by the terms of the peace treaty to give up Natal and a strip of land across the Tugela River in Zululand. Other trekkers settled farther north at Lydenberg, Ohrigstad, and Soutpansberg, from where they were later expelled by the Venda. In the face of such resistance, the Boers opted to settle south of the Tugela, and founded the Republic of Natalia, the Orange Free State, and the Transvaal.

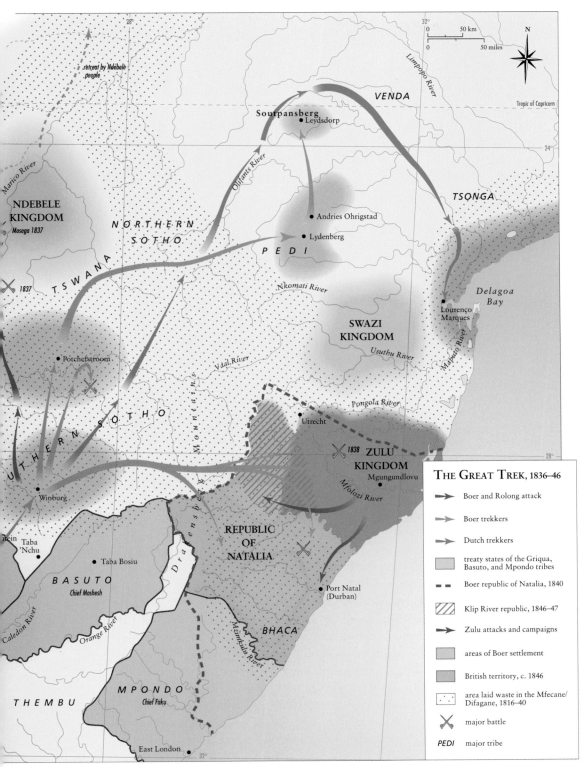

retreat by Ndebele
people

VENDA

Limpopo River

Tropic of Capricorn

Soutpansberg
• Leydsdorp

Marico River

**NDEBELE
KINGDOM**
Mosega 1837

**NORTHERN
SOTHO**

Olifants River

TSONGA

✕ 1837

T S W A N A

P E D I

• Andries Ohrigstad

• Lydenberg

*Delagoa
Bay*

Nkomati River

• Lourenço
Marques

Maputo River

**SWAZI
KINGDOM**

Usuthu River

• Potchefstroom

Vaal River

✕

Pongola River

• Utrecht

S O U T H E R N   S O T H O

D r a k e n s b e r g   M o u n t a i n s

✕ 1838 **ZULU
KINGDOM**
• Mgungundlovu

Mfolozi River

• Winburg

cin Taba
'Nchu

• Taba Bosiu

**REPUBLIC
OF
NATALIA**

✕

B A S U T O
Chief Moshesh

Caledon River

Orange River

Mzimkulu River

• Port Natal
(Durban)

B H A C A

T H E M B U

M P O N D O
Chief Faku

• East London

THE GREAT TREK, 1836–46	
➤	Boer and Rolong attack
→	Boer trekkers
→	Dutch trekkers
▢	treaty states of the Griqua, Basuto, and Mpondo tribes
- - -	Boer republic of Natalia, 1840
▨	Klip River republic, 1846–47
→	Zulu attacks and campaigns
▨	areas of Boer settlement
▨	British territory, c. 1846
⋰	area laid waste in the Mfecane/ Difagane, 1816–40
✕	major battle
PEDI	major tribe

0   50 km
0   50 miles

N

THE BOER WARS

Three generations of Boers at war: P. J. Lemmer, 65, J. L. Botha, 15, and G. I. Pretorius, 43. The war lasted from 1899 to 1902, pressing Boer manpower to exhaustion and costing Britain and its empire some 30,000 casualties.

The wars were not the black Africans' wars but were a struggle between two European imperialist communities to determine which group had the real power in the region. Change in South Africa came about when a new Unionist (Conservative) government led by Lord Salisbury came into office in Britain. This new government was determined to impose its authority over the Transvaal, especially regarding its railway links to Cape Colony, but Jameson's raid of 1895 undermined the efforts of the South African prime minister to negotiate with the Transvaal authorities.

The appointment in 1897 of Alfred Milner as high commissioner to South Africa marked a turning point in Anglo-Boer relations. Milner, in order to gain access and control of the mining interests in the Transvaal, demanded reform and threatened war. His diplomatic maneuvering to create opposition to the Transvaal's president, Kruger, and his dealings with the South African League, annoyed the Boers. Other antagonistic appointments included those of Chamberlain to the Colonial Office and of W. P. Schreiner as prime minister of the Colony. When negotiations between Milner, Kruger, and the Boer general, Smuts, broke down, the Boers declared war, believing they had an advantage over the British; Smuts had 40,000 men, compared to the 15,000 in the British garrisons. Commandos from the Orange Free State who had fought in the wars against blacks for Transvaal independence joined the war by moving to Natal. The Boers intended to move against Cape Colony and start rebellions in Durban, Kimberley, Ladysmith, Vryburg, and Cape Town, the railway nerve centers. After mismanagement of the campaign, Lord Roberts took control of the British forces from General R. Butler. British commanders reacted to the Boer guerilla tactics with brutality, burning farms, pillaging, and imprisoning all members of the Boer population.

Injustice and brutality became so widespread during the war that women in the Cape organized an opposition movement to protest against the colonial government. Train wrecking was common, and Boers caught wearing British military uniforms were executed. Boers in turn stole farm animals and coerced neutral blacks into acting as carriers and spies. Concentration camps were introduced for the first time when the British cordoned off large areas of South Africa under the pretext of rounding up the rebels, and similar camps came to be used tactically to bring an end to the war. In May 1900 General Brabat suggested the establishment of protected camps for surrendering Boers, and Kitchener put the idea into practice. Once these were erected, they also included refugees seeking British protection, families of fighting Boers forced into the camps in the Cape Colony and Natal.

The most famous encounter of the war was the siege of Mafeking, which lasted for seven months from October 1889. The siege came to feature heroically in British mythology, partly thanks to the publicism of Colonel Baden-Powell, but in truth the Africans in Mafeking were mistreated and denied food, while their white counterparts were fed.

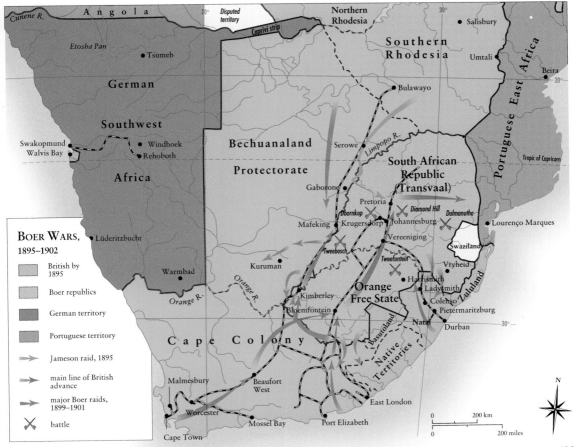

BOER WARS, 1895–1902

- British by 1895
- Boer republics
- German territory
- Portuguese territory
- Jameson raid, 1895
- main line of British advance
- major Boer raids, 1899–1901
- battle

PART IV: THE AFRICAN DIASPORA

Apart from recent emigrants, most Africans living outside Africa today are the descendants of slaves whose diaspora covers a period of nearly 2,000 years. African slaves were recorded in the ninth century BC to be living in India, China, and Persia, where they were employed to dig saltpeter. During their occupation of Britain, the Romans imported the first Africans to settle in the islands. As early as the Tang dynasty (AD 712), slaves were transported to China, where they became servants or, as Duan Chengshi recorded, herdsmen, and supplemented China's labor needs in domestic and military service. In the Middle East, wealthy Muslims transported slaves across the Sahara and women were commonly sold as domestic servants. When the Crusaders occupied Palestine and Syria, they inherited slaves who worked on Muslim-owned sugar plantations. As early as 1300, when Cyprus became the major sugar-growing country in the Mediterranean, it hosted the busiest slave market. Long before the transatlantic trade, Africans were sold to Europeans to work as domestic slaves or as miners, and in many parts of the world it was a mark of class to own a black servant. In India, for example, in the sixteenth and seventeenth centuries, African slaves known as Coffrees were status symbols.

The chief strands in the more recent, mainly transatlantic diaspora include

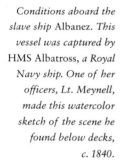

Conditions aboard the slave ship Albanez. *This vessel was captured by* HMS Albatross, *a Royal Navy ship. One of her officers, Lt. Meynell, made this watercolor sketch of the scene he found below decks, c. 1840.*

African Americans (North and South America), African-Caribbeans, British and French Africans, and other widespread African exiles. By contrast with the Middle East, in the Americas, the populations of African slaves were often larger than those of their white masters, and they provided the major source of domestic and plantation labor, where their role was to produce commodities for export to Europe and elsewhere.

African chiefs controlled the supply of slaves to the Europeans from western and southwestern Africa, and the majority of the enslaved people, who included women, children, and outcasts, were captured by Africans in civil wars or raids. Those taken to America and the West Indies were chained and packed in ships, which took up to four months to cross the Atlantic. Available records of this Middle Passage speak of the terrible suffering endured by the slaves and of their resulting high mortality rate. Although they were shackled in the holds beneath the decks, crews watched for violence and revolts, against which harsh retribution was meted. To reduce the risk of rebellion, ship owners improved security by building shelves which allowed their captives little or no movement.

Wherever there was a high concentration of slaves, revolts and violence were

"Made a timely discovery today that the slaves were forming a plot for insurrection. Surprised two of them attempting to get their irons off. . . . Put the boys in irons and slightly in the thumbscrews to urge them to a full confession." *Captain Newton,* of the ship Duke of Argyle, 1751

common. Surviving Persian and Arab writers such as al-Tabari record a string of Zanj (Arabic for black) slave revolts and subsequent massacres from as early as AD 689. Slaves pitted themselves against the Persian army and rioted at Basra, paying with their lives. Africans rebeled on ships in transit as well as at their places of destination, and revolts were commonplace in Spanish territories in the Caribbean and in Central and South America. Often slaves tried to avenge the violence of their white masters, organizing gangs, like the Maroons in Jamaica who in 1739 forced the British to recognize them as free men. In 1761 the Dutch were similarly forced to make peace with their rebellious slaves in Surinam.

The plan and section of a slave ship; the inset sketch (right) shows a slave insurrection in progress. From their position in the stern the crew opened fire on the hapless captives. Some of the slaves leapt over-board, preferring death to enslavement.

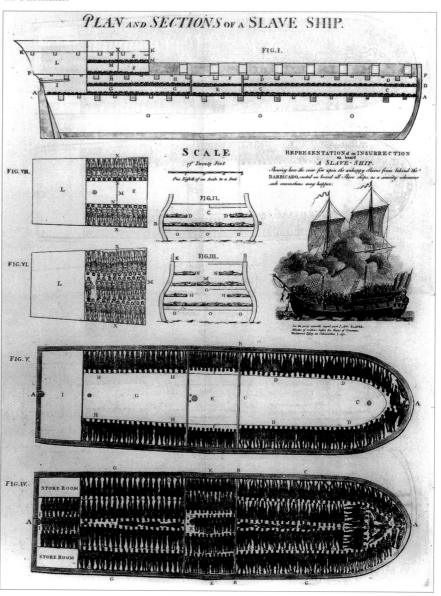

The African populations in the New World grew as the slave-based economies boosted their exports—especially of sugar, tobacco, cotton, coffee, and cocoa—back to Europe. In mid eighteenth-century England, for example, London had about five hundred coffee houses, which functioned as social meeting places for its residents and absentee planters; black slaves were often auctioned in such premises. New seaports, too, like Liverpool and Bristol, owed their development to the slave trade.

Toussaint l'Ouverture was born in Africa sometime in the 1740s and was captured by slavers and transported to Haiti. As he grew older, he learned, with the approval of his master, to read, devouring the classic works of his age. He steadily rose in position and eventually became butler to his plantation owner. He joined the great slave uprising (only after helping his master to escape), and with his gifts of language and education soon rose to command. Initially he allied himself with Spain, but with the revolution in France, he changed his loyalties. He defeated a British invasion, installing himself as ruler of the whole island from 1801. Meanwhile, after the Peace of Amiens, France sent an army to reclaim the island. After a bloody and largely unsuccessful struggle, the French commander artfully drew Toussaint into peaceful negotiations and then seized and transported him to France, where he died a prisoner in the Fortress of Joux in 1803.

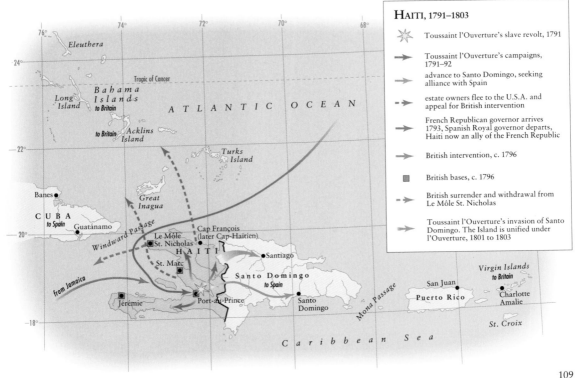

HAITI, 1791–1803

Toussaint l'Ouverture's slave revolt, 1791

Toussaint l'Ouverture's campaigns, 1791–92

advance to Santo Domingo, seeking alliance with Spain

estate owners flee to the U.S.A. and appeal for British intervention

French Republican governor arrives 1793, Spanish Royal governor departs, Haiti now an ally of the French Republic

British intervention, c. 1796

British bases, c. 1796

British surrender and withdrawal from Le Môle St. Nicholas

Toussaint l'Ouverture's invasion of Santo Domingo. The Island is unified under l'Ouverture, 1801 to 1803

THE AMERICAS

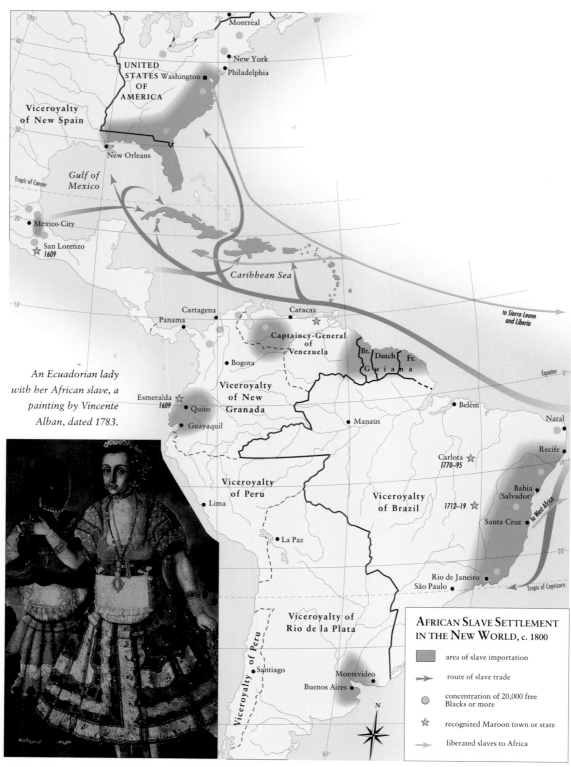

UNITED STATES OF AMERICA Washington

Viceroyalty of New Spain

Montréal

New York

Philadelphia

Gulf of Mexico

New Orleans

Tropic of Cancer

Mexico City

San Lorenzo
1609

Caribbean Sea

An Ecuadorian lady with her African slave, a painting by Vincente Alban, dated 1783.

Cartagena

Panama

Caracas

Captaincy-General of Venezuela

Bogota

Esmeralda
1609

Quito

Guayaquil

Viceroyalty of New Granada

Br. Dutch Fr.
Guiana

to Sierra Leone
and Liberia

Equator

Belém

Manaus

Natal

Recife

Carlota
1770–95

Bahia
(Salvador)

Viceroyalty of Peru

Lima

Viceroyalty of Brazil

1712–19

Santa Cruz

to West Africa

La Paz

Rio de Janeiro

São Paulo

Tropic of Capricorn

Viceroyalty of Peru

Viceroyalty of Rio de la Plata

Santiago

Montevideo

Buenos Aires

N

AFRICAN SLAVE SETTLEMENT IN THE NEW WORLD, c. 1800

- area of slave importation
- route of slave trade
- concentration of 20,000 free Blacks or more
- ☆ recognized Maroon town or state
- liberated slaves to Africa

A street scene in the market square in St. Georges, Grenada Island. The majority of the population of the Caribbean is of African descent.

SLAVE AND FREE BLACKS IN THE CARIBBEAN, EARLY 19TH CENTURY

Total population, in thousands

- 1,000
- 500
- 250
- 100

Population composition

- free blacks
- slaves
- whites

The spread of plantations throughout the Americas matched that of African communities, and the slaves also supplied vital labor for mines and provided valuable weaving and ironmaking skills. By 1800, the white populations of Virginia, Maryland, and North and South Carolina were relying on the Africans for the production of their wealth from tobacco, cotton, and other crops. Brazil was home to over two million Africans, most of whom were domestic servants or slave laborers on coffee plantations or in mines. Elsewhere in South America, the West Indies, and islands such as Cuba, Puerto Rico, Haiti, and Santo Domingo, the immigrants were typically put to work on sugar cane or banana plantations, to which they brought their specialist agricultural expertise from tropical Africa. Slaves were also imported in numbers into Colombia, Venezuela, New Granada, and Guiana. Around 400,000 served in the military across Spanish America.

By the early nineteenth century, African slaves were beginning to breed and multiply in sufficient numbers to render their further importation to the New World unnecessary, and under pressure from European humanitarians like William Wilberforce, slavery was officially abolished throughout the British empire by the Act of 1833. The impact of abolition varied with geographical location, for by this time close-knit slave communities had been created throughout the Caribbean. In the West Indies, some slaves who chose to leave the plantations migrated to Cuba and to Central America to find work while others joined the growing population of black sailors from West Africa. In America some freed slaves stayed on the plantations and became sharecroppers.

Although the slaves worked with their foreign masters to build new civilizations in new lands, many never lost their Africanness, imparting not only their practical skills but also their shared cultural heritage to their new communities. Their mixed African origins sometimes catalyzed quite new diasporic cultures. For example, patois languages such as Creole and Gullah are syntheses of several African and European languages. Traditional African religions absorbed elements of Christianity, evident in the voodoo and Santeria cults of Haiti and Cuba. Africans also contributed to new forms of folklore and the arts. The Anansi tales from Ghana, for instance, survived and were adapted to new cultural and political experiences in the West Indies and Britain. African traditions and experiences were keys to the creation of spiritual and gospel music and of blues and jazz in the United States, a heritage that in the twentieth century has generated a worldwide popular music.

Today over ninety million people in the Americas are of African origin, among whom the most dynamic and politicized are those of the United States, scene in the 1960s of an intense civil rights struggle. In modern Britain the largest single non-white group is formed by West Indians who have reemigrated. From the slaves' enforced diaspora there have grown new and dynamic African-American and African-Caribbean cultures.

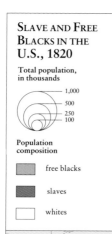

SLAVE AND FREE BLACKS IN THE U.S., 1820

Total population, in thousands

- 1,000
- 500
- 250
- 100

Population composition

- free blacks
- slaves
- whites

Frederick Douglass, born a slave in 1817, escaped from his Maryland owner in 1838 and sailed to Britain. He later returned to the United States and purchased his freedom. A tireless antislavery campaigner, Douglass issued a call for the formation of black units in the Union Army during the Civil War and helped organize two regiments. He died in 1895 after holding many government posts.

"I have a dream that one day the sons of former slaves and the sons of former slave owners will be able to sit together at the table of brotherhood."
Martin Luther King, Jr., 1963

Provost Guard of the 107th Colored Infantry, photographed at Fort Corcoran, part of the Union forces deployed in the defense of Washington, D.C.

113

EURASIA

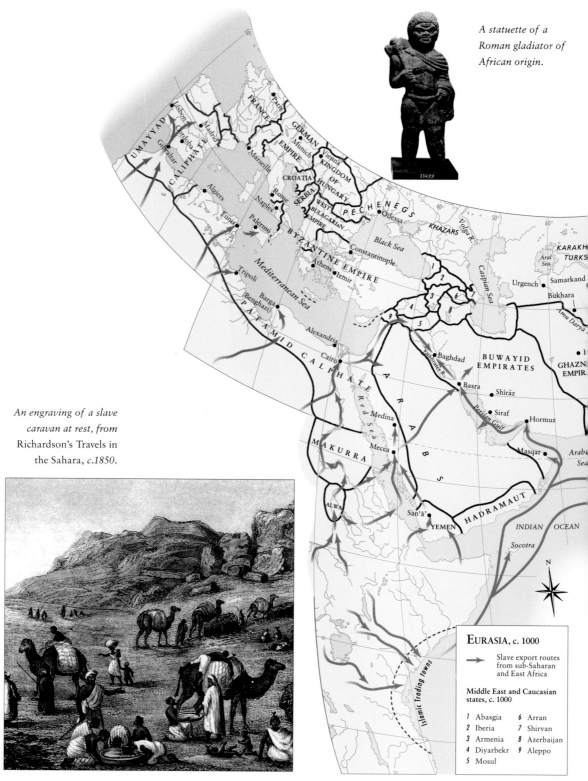

A statuette of a Roman gladiator of African origin.

An engraving of a slave caravan at rest, from Richardson's Travels in the Sahara, c.1850.

Paris

UMAYYAD

CALIPHATE

Lisbon
Córdoba
Madrid
Gibraltar

FRANCE

GERMAN
EMPIRE
Munich
Vienna

KINGDOM
OF
HUNGARY

CROATIA

SERBIA

WEST
BULGARIAN
EMPIRE

PECHENEGS

Marseille
Rome
Naples
Palermo

Algiers
Tunis

Tripoli

Barqa
Benghazi
P Y R A M I D   C A L I P H A T E

Mediterranean Sea

BYZANTINE EMPIRE
Athens
Izmir
Constantinople

Black Sea

Odessa

KHAZARS

Volga R.

Caspian Sea

KARAKH
TURKS

Aral
Sea

Urgench
Samarkand

Bukhara

Amu Darya

1
2
3
9
4
5
6
7
8

Alexandria
Cairo

Euphrates R.
Baghdad
Basra

BUWAYID
EMPIRES

Shīrāz
Sīrāf
Hormuz

GHAZN
EMPIR

A R A B S

Red Sea

Medina
Mecca

Persian Gulf

Masqat

Arab
Sea

MAKURRA

ALWA

San'a'
YEMEN

HADRAMAUT

INDIAN   OCEAN

Socotra

N

Islamic Trading towns

EURASIA, c. 1000

→ Slave export routes from sub-Saharan and East Africa

Middle East and Caucasian states, c. 1000

1 Abasgia	6 Arran
2 Iberia	7 Shirvan
3 Armenia	8 Azerbaijan
4 Diyarbekr	9 Aleppo
5 Mosul	

For many centuries Africans have been transported across the Sahara, the Red Sea, the Indian Ocean, and along the Nile. Unlike the Atlantic slave trade, which is well recorded, figures for this more ancient traffic are not well quantified. Around the ninth century, the trade increased after the Arab conquest of North Africa brought improved trans-Saharan routes, and until the nineteenth century an average of 6,000 slaves a year were brought through the desert. While a large proportion of slaves transported to the Americas were male, those taken across the Sahara were predominantly female. The women usually became wives or concubines serving in Arab harems, and young males were usually castrated to become eunuchs, explaining the low numbers of recorded African descendants. Women and children were assimilated into Islamic society, for if a woman gave birth she was protected from resale to another master, and her children became free citizens. By the ninth century the Islamic world was the foremost importer of slaves, mostly captured in jihads, and throughout the Middle East large contingents of Africans did manual jobs like working in slate mines or serving in the military. The Arab writer al-Muqaddasi notes that at one time there were 7,000 eunuchs in Baghdad alone. There are records of slave uprisings in Basra and Baghdad in 689, 869, and 871.

From about 800, trade in slaves from the Red Sea and the Indian Ocean coast is said to have averaged about 3,000 a year. Of these, many thousands may have been transported to China and India.

The East African coast was famous, and merchants from India and China traveled there to exchange manufactured goods for slaves, who fetched high prices back home. It was prestigious, for example, to have a bodyguard of African origin. The presence of African slaves in India was recorded by Captain Henry Bevan, who in 1831 recounted how he had been approached by Africans wanting to join his corps in Goa. In Ceylon the Dutch imported African slaves to work on the plantations.

Evidence of African civilization in Europe is most evident in southern Spain. As early as the eighth century, Berber Muslims in Andalusia founded settlements, brought with them farming, building, and weaving skills, and established a civilization that survived until the Spanish reconquest in the fourteenth century. Andalusia was ruled first by Abd al-Rahman, born of Berber and Arabic parents, and later by leaders of the Almoravid and Almohad dynasties from northwest Africa. Among their lasting monuments is the mosque at Cordoba. Andalusia also produced scholars like al-Bakri, the great traveler who in 1097 wrote his celebrated Book of the Roads and Kingdoms. The first slaves later to be taken to Portugal, in 1441, were for the amusement of Prince Henry. The Venetians used slaves to grow sugar in their colonies, especially in the largest, on the island of Crete.

Mocha, at the southern end of the Red Sea, was one of the many staging posts in the slave trade between Africa and Asia.

By the mid fourteenth century, Africans reached Europe as ambassadors or visitors from states such as Benin and Congo. Examples of the African presence

in Europe are to be found in paintings by German and Italian artists that represent black attendants, like the servant in Gozzoli's Journey of Magi of 1461. In England Africans became members of the court of King James IV.

After the fifteenth century, African slaves continued to be exported by Arabs across the Sahara and from the East African coast, while Europeans operated the markets in the rest of Africa. In East Africa, after the Arabs wrested the control of the coast back from the Portuguese, they traveled into the interior to capture slaves in order to supply the growing markets in the Middle and Far East, and India. While Khartoum Arabs raided northern Uganda and Kenya for slaves for the Egyptian army, Zanzibari and Swahili Arabs, and Indians based at Kilwa and Zanzibar controlled the trade on the coast. Long-distance caravans, each containing some 1,000 men—mainly slaves carrying copper and ivory—were used by Arabs to travel from the interior to the coast. Mirambo, chief of the Nyamwezi in Tanganyika, and Muhammed bin Sayed, popularly known as Tippu Tip, are reputed to have been the greatest slave traders in Africa. Their total depopulation of the land between Lake Malawi and the coast was a terrible warning of how disastrous the trade would become for the rest of the continent.

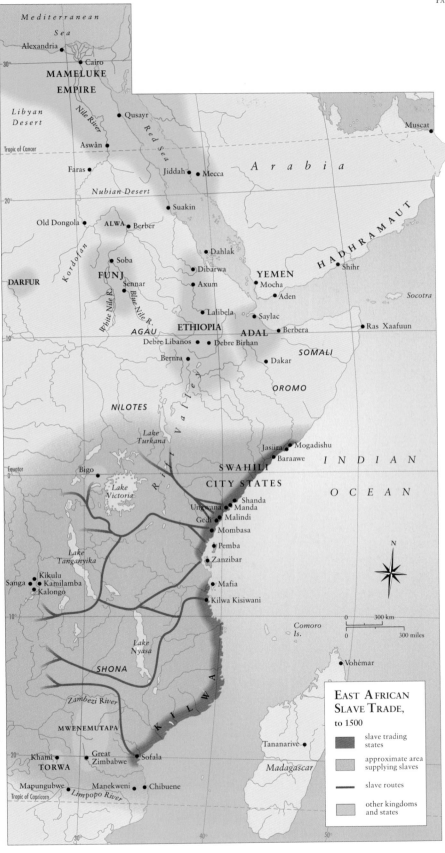

Mediterranean Sea
Alexandria
Cairo
MAMELUKE
EMPIRE
Libyan Desert
Nile River
Qusayr
Tropic of Cancer
Aswân
Faras
Jiddah
Mecca
Arabia
Nubian Desert
Suakin
Old Dongola
ALWA
Berber
Muscat
Red Sea
Dahlak
HADHRAMAUT
Soba
Dibarwa
YEMEN
Shihr
DARFUR
FUNJ
Sennar
Axum
Mocha
Aden
Socotra
Lalibela
Saylac
Berbera
Ras Xaafuun
AGAU
ETHIOPIA
ADAL
Debre Libanos
Debre Birhan
SOMALI
Bernra
Dakar
NILOTES
OROMO
Kordofan
White Nile R.
Blue Nile R.
Rift Valley
Lake Turkana
Jasiira
Mogadishu
Baraawe
INDIAN
Equator
Bigo
SWAHILI
CITY STATES
OCEAN
Lake Victoria
Shanda
Ungwana
Manda
Gedi
Malindi
Mombasa
N
Lake Tanganyika
Pemba
Zanzibar
Kikulu
Kamilamba
Sanga
Kalongo
Mafia
Kilwa Kisiwani
Comoro Is.
0   300 km
0   300 miles
SHONA
Lake Nyasa
Vohémar
Zambezi River
KILWA
EAST AFRICAN
SLAVE TRADE,
to 1500
MWENEMUTAPA
Tananarive
Khami
Great Zimbabwe
Sofala
TORWA
Madagascar
slave trading states
Mapungubwe
Manekweni
Chibuene
Limpopo River
Tropic of Capricorn
approximate area supplying slaves
slave routes
other kingdoms and states

"Probably the slave trade along the roads of Kordofan had never been so flourishing. Neither Baker nor the Government accomplished anything like a practical supervision over the local authorities." *Dr. Georg August Schweinfurth,* explorer and naturalist, c. 1870.

PART V: IMPERIALISM TO INDEPENDENCE

Colonial occupation took many different forms. In areas like Kenya, Rhodesia (Zimbabwe), and South Africa, white settlers appropriated the land of the native inhabitants, imposing direct rule. This usually meant pushing the former occupants into reserves mostly located on unproductive land and exploiting their labor in large, foreign-owned plantations or mines. But Africans were not always ready to surrender their land and independence, and the colonizers often had to resort to force to secure effective control. Violent resistance was the hallmark of the period between initial imperial invasion and pacification.

In West Africa, because of active resistance, the colonialists, especially the British, found it hard to settle the land, and various other indirect methods were employed to impose imperial rule. The idea of indirect rule, associated with Lord Lugard, was that local chiefs should be employed to administer the day-to-day running of the territories, and be entrusted with the responsibility to keep order. This was thought to be an economical method, but was widely abused as attempts were made to create new chiefdoms where none had previously existed.

While the Germans, Portuguese, and Belgians employed direct rule, the French attempted assimilation, but both methods involved the destruction of traditional authorities, the introduction of alien, centralized, authoritarian systems, and the appointment of foreign agents to rule the territories.

After the First World War, the British hold on Egypt and elsewhere was for a while strengthened, and Africa was repartitioned, but the war's lasting effect was a general dismantling of the power and mystique of the white colonial masters. By the beginning of the Second World War, African resistance to occupation had created many political organizations led by educated Africans, whose interest became stimulated in interregional cooperation, and when the war ended the major European occupiers became more concerned with the economic and social development of their colonies. The Sixth Pan-African Conference held in Manchester, England, in 1945 emphasized the urgency of overthrowing colonial governments and demanded equal justice, freedom of expression, and democracy throughout the continent.

First the North African countries—Libya, Morocco, and Tunisia—achieved independence from Italy, and France in 1951, 1955, and 1956 respectively. South of the Sahara, Ghana became independent from Britain in 1957 and Nigeria in 1960. Where nations were denied political independence, nationalist guerilla movements were initiated to uproot the colonialists.

Land had always been an emotional issue in Africa, a fact well illustrated by the protracted and bloody Mau-Mau war fought by Kenya's Kikuyus against the British. Conflict broke out after the Second World War between the white settlers and the disinherited Kikuyus, led by Jomo Kenyatta (1891–1978). The war started in 1952 and lasted for four years, and though disturbances continued, the colonial government was victorious, the settlers' grip on Kenya was shaken, and the country gained independence in 1963.

The Portuguese were eventually expelled from Angola, Cape Verde, Guinea

Nairobi, capital of Kenya, was cris-crossed with barbed wire and barricades during the Mau-Mau crisis, 1952–1956.

(Guinea-Bissau), and Mozambique by similar movements. In Angola the Movimento Popular de Libertaçao de Angola (MPLA) took power, and in Mozambique the Frente de Libertaçao de Mozambique (FRELIMO). In former Rhodesia, the Zimbabwe African National Union (ZANU) won the war, and Rhodesia, renamed Zimbabwe became independent in April 1980.

After the Portuguese withdrawal from Angola and Mozambique in 1975, Africa embarked on a second phase of liberation. Despite decolonization, many African communities became frustrated by leaders who were unwilling to deliver them the rightful fruits *(matunda)* of independence. For many peasants nothing changed, as constitutional governments became political dictatorships, especially when their leaders turned them into one-party states or one-man fiefs. Secessionist movements too were often badly mismanaged. In Zaire, for example, the Katanga uprising resulted in the coup d'état staged by Mobutu in 1965. In 1966 Biafra announced its secession from Nigeria, and the bloody civil war that followed lasted until 1970. National independence sometimes became the catalyst of ethnic conflict, as witnessed in Uganda in 1966 and in Burundi and Rwanda in 1972 and 1989.

The predominantly Ibo region of southwest Nigeria, fearful of Hausa domination, broke away to form the republic of Biafra in 1967. Here, rebel soldiers stand guard at a river crossing.

While the rest of Africa celebrated independence, between 1957 and 1990 South Africa remained under the rule of a white minority government. Following the end of the Anglo-Boer war of 1899–1902, African nationalists formed the African National Congress (ANC). The industrialization of South Africa after the outbreak of the Second World War increased the country's dependence on migrant black labor, and the construction of the apartheid ideology politicized the segregated black laborers, who were forced to live on reserves. The period between 1960 and 1989 was characterized by frequently violent campaigns against the apartheid regime which climaxed with the recognition of the ANC, the release of its leader Nelson Mandela after twenty-seven years in prison, democratic elections, and in 1994 the installation of a black majority government.

From the time of independence African states have struggled to set up interstate trading organizations with the aim of promoting economic cooperation and political stability. The Organization of African Unity (OAU), formed in 1963, is the umbrella organization that aims to promote harmony and common policies among its member countries, while the Commonwealth brings together states formerly ruled by the British.

The Nigerian federal government was determined to destroy the breakaway republic of Biafra. They drove the rebels into a small enclave, and by 1970 Biafra ceased to exist. Here, government troops examine captured munitions.

AFRICAN RESISTANCE

Early African resistance to the European colonialists was scattered across the continent, and included the Ashanti wars in Ghana, the Zulu wars in South Africa, the Ndebele-Shona wars in Rhodesia, Kabarega's and Mwanga's wars in Uganda, the Hehe wars in Tanganyika (German East Africa), and the Nandi and Giriama wars in Kenya and the Niger Delta. Later, there was the Maji-Maji rebellion in Tanganyika (1898–1914), the Mau-Mau rebellion of the 1950s in Kenya, and the Adamawa emirates' rebellion in Cameroon. Resistance also occurred in the form of religious wars, such as Sultan Attahiru Ahmadu's Hijra against the British in Sokoto, Sayyed Muhammad Hassan's jihad of 1899–1920 against the British in Somalia, Mahmadou Lane's against the French in Senegal, and Mandinka emperor Samori Toure's against the French during the 1880s and 1890s.

In eastern, central, and southern Africa, where control of European territories was first administered by chartered companies, bitter struggles continued for years. Along the East African coast there was the Mazrui rebellion of 1895–1896, led by Mbaruk, against A. H. Hardinge's British control of the coastal strip; this involved both the Arabs and twelve African tribes, including the Giriama and Mijikenda, but was eventually suppressed with the help of troops from India. Germans met with stiff resistance along the coast and in the interior of Tanganyika, where the Yao of the Makonde plains and the Unyanyembe rebelled. Mkwawa, chief of the Hehe, who were united by the Ngoni invasions of the 1840s, also rose against the Germans between 1891 and 1894, when his capital at Kalenga was destroyed. He then waged a guerilla war until his death in 1898.

The "Great Powers" deployed large numbers of their national armies on duties overseas. Here the British 91st infantry regiment drills in the South African sun. Photographed in 1879.

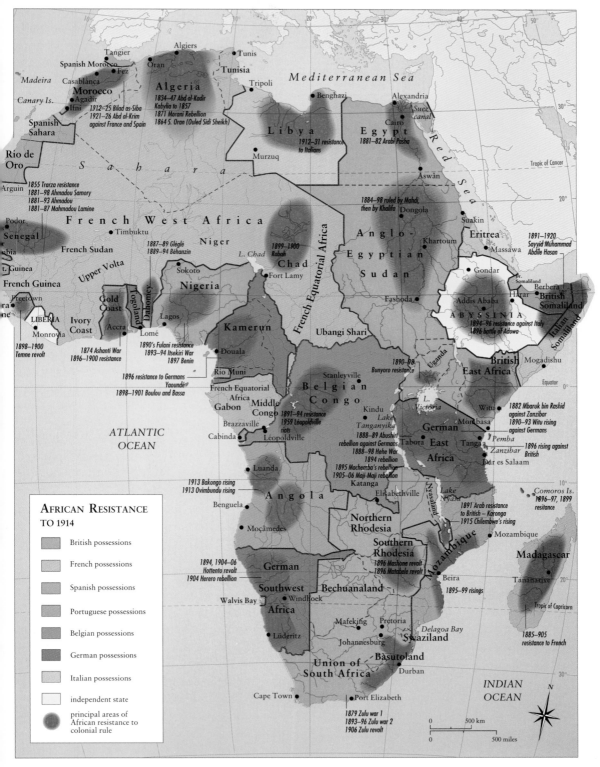

Tangier
Algiers
Tunis
Spanish Morocco
Oran
Tunisia
Madeira
Fez
Tripoli
Casablanca
Mediterranean Sea
Alexandria
Canary Is.
Morocco
Agadir
Algeria
Benghazi
Suez canal
Ifni
1912–25 Bilad as-Siba
1921–26 Abd al-Krim against France and Spain
1834–47 Abd al-Kadir Kabylia to 1857
1871 Morani Rebellion
1864 S. Oran (Ouled Sidi Sheikh)
Cairo
Egypt
Spanish Sahara
Libya
1881–82 Arabi Pasha
Río de Oro
1912–31 resistance to Italians
Murzuq
Red Sea
Tropic of Cancer
S a h a r a
Aswân
Arguin
1855 Trarza resistance
1881–98 Ahmadou Samory
1881–93 Ahmadou
1881–87 Mahmadou Lamine
1884–98 ruled by Mahdi, then by Khalifa
Dongola
Suakin
Podor
Senegal
F r e n c h   W e s t   A f r i c a
Timbuktu
Niger
A n g l o -
Khartoum
Eritrea
Massawa
1891–1920 Sayyid Muhammad Abdile Hasan
abia
French Sudan
L. Chad
1899–1900 Rabah
E g y p t i a n
t. Guinea
Upper Volta
1887–89 Glégé
1889–94 Béhanzin
Chad
Sokoto
Fort Lamy
Gondar
Somaliland
Berbera
French Guinea
Togoland
Dahomey
Nigeria
S u d a n
Fashoda
Addis Ababa
Harar
British Somaliland
eetown
Gold Coast
Lagos
A B Y S S I N I A
1894–96 resistance against Italy
1896 battle of Adowa
ne
LIBERIA
Ivory Coast
Accra
Lomé
Kamerun
French Equatorial Africa
Ubangi Shari
Monrovia
1898–1900 Temne revolt
1874 Ashanti War
1896–1900 resistance
1890's Fulani resistance
1893–94 Itsekiri War
1897 Benin
Douala
1890–98 Bunyoro resistance
Mogadishu
Italian Somaliland
1896 resistance to Germans
Yaoundé
1898–1901 Boulou and Bassa
Rio Muni
Stanleyville
B e l g i a n
Uganda
British East Africa
Equator
French Equatorial Africa
Gabon
Middle Congo
1891–94 resistance
1959 Léopoldville riots
C o n g o
Kindu
Lake Victoria
1882 Mbaruk bin Rashid against Zanzibar
1890–93 Witu rising against Germans
Witu
ATLANTIC OCEAN
Brazzaville
Cabinda
Léopoldville
Lake Tanganyika
German
Tabora
East
Mombasa
Pemba
1896 rising against British
1888–89 Abushiri rebellion against Germans
1888–98 Hehe War
1894 rebellion
1895 Machemba's rebellion
1905–06 Maji-Maji rebellion
Africa
Tanga
Zanzibar
Dar es Salaam
Luanda
Katanga
Elisabethville
1913 Bakongo rising
1913 Ovimbundu rising
A n g o l a
Lake Nyasa
Comoros Is.
1896–97, 1899 resistance
AFRICAN RESISTANCE
TO 1914
Benguela
Northern Rhodesia
1891 Arab resistance to British – Karonga
1915 Chilembwe's rising
Moçâmedes
Mozambique
Mozambique
Madagascar
British possessions
Southern Rhodesia
Tananarive
French possessions
1894, 1904–06 Hottento revolt
1904 Herero rebellion
German
1896 Mashona revolt
1896 Matabele revolt
Spanish possessions
Southwest
Bechuanaland
Beira
Portuguese possessions
Africa
Walvis Bay
Windhoek
1895–99 risings
Tropic of Capricorn
Belgian possessions
Mafeking
Pretoria
Delagoa Bay
1885–905 resistance to French
German possessions
Lüderitz
Johannesburg
Swaziland
Italian possessions
Union of South Africa
Basutoland
independent state
Durban
INDIAN OCEAN
principal areas of African resistance to colonial rule
Cape Town
Port Elizabeth
1879 Zulu war 1
1893–96 Zulu war 2
1906 Zulu revolt
0   500 km
0   500 miles

Along the Mrima coast in 1888, a fierce Swahili resistance movement led by Bushiri bin Salim and Bwana Heri destabilized Karl Peters' German administration in Tanganyika (German East Africa). The rebellion forced the German government to take over German companies' properties in Tanganyika. The Maji Maji rebellion in the Tanganyika interior was part of secondary resistance against the taxation, forced labor, and economic malpractice inflicted by colonial rule. Mutinies involving African mercenaries occurred in Cameroon in 1893, when the police force ejected German administrators from Cameroon.

British sailors open fire on an outraged Egyptian crowd in Alexandria, 1882.

In the northeast African interior, a Sudanese fakir, Muhammad Ahmad, in 1882 declared himself a Mahdi ("The Guided One") and organized a rebellion in 1894 against Anglo-Egyptian rule in central Sudan, while the British, the French, and the Belgians were busy sharing the area around Lake Chad, Rabih ibn Fadl Allah, a veteran of the Egyptian campaign, played a central part in resistance; he established himself in Bornu, and fought against the French until his defeat at the battle of Lakhata in 1900.

African resistance in West Africa continued for a long time, especially by the Ibo and Tiv peoples of Mali, Niger, the Ivory Coast, and Mauritania. While in Sokoto the Caliphate fell to Lugard's army, in other areas leaders such as Samori Toure and Bai Bureh in Sierra Leone sustained guerilla wars long after their territories had been conquered.

In the Maghrib, the French were resisted by Abd al-Karim of Morocco, who was not defeated until 1933. Abd al-Orim fought against the Spanish and the French in the Rif (1921–1926), the Sanusi Bedouins warred against the Italians in Tripolitania (1912–1931), the Egyptians fought the British (1919–1920), and Sayyid Muhammad led the Somalis against the British, Italians, and Ethiopians (1891–1920). In 1913, the Portuguese faced two uprisings by the Bailundo of Bakongo and Ovimbundu. Farther south the Germans experienced their worst resistance in Africa when the Hehe revolted in 1904, followed by the Hottentots. In Madagascar, local people rose against the Hova and the French, but their rebellion was crushed. The Ndebele and the Shona rose against the colonialists in 1893 and 1896, but they too were defeated.

In the Sudan, the Mahdi, "The Guided One," and the Muslim revivalists led a major revolt, taking control over most of the Egyptian dependency of the Sudan in 1885. The Mahdi remained undefeated until the Battle of Omdurman, on September 2, 1898, when an Anglo-Egyptian force destroyed his army.

AFRICA IN WORLD WAR I

In northern Africa, the British strengthened their hold on Egypt in order to use it as a base to spark off revolts in the Arab territories against the weakening Ottoman empire. When Italy's invasion of Libya triggered an attempted rebellion by the Islamic Sanusi order (backed by Ottoman support), British troops appropriated Egyptian resources to buttress their Italian allies in a successful campaign against the rebels.

From early on in the war, the allies launched operations against German colonies in Africa. In South Africa, a pro-German faction of the Boer population rebelled against the British colonial administration in an attempt to offset an invasion of German Southwest Africa by government forces. In eastern Africa there were extensive allied campaigns; German colonies were overrun, and became mandated territories of the League of Nations following the war.

African soldiers serving in the French army sought out captured equipment on the western front, in France, July 1918.

Many Africans fought in Europe, and most of the soldiers used by Britain, France, Belgium, and South Africa in World War I to fight against the Germans in Africa were black. They fought in the German territories of Southwest Africa, German East Africa (Tanganyika, Rwanda, and Burundi), Togo, and Cameroon. They were partnered in Southwest Africa by white South Africans, and in German East Africa by Indians. The African Northern Rhodesia Rifles fought along the Caprivi Strip, Abercorn, and the northeast frontier, to defend the country against invading German forces. In Nyasaland, which bordered German East Africa, about 20,000 joined the King's African Rifles, while other Africans fought in the north. Kenya alone contributed over 10,000 soldiers and 195,000 porters. In 1916 a hut and poll tax was levied in Kenya and Uganda to help meet the war costs and Africans also supplied food and cattle.

The bloody war to occupy German East Africa witnessed the death of about 4,000 African soldiers and 30,000 supply porters and roadmakers recruited both by the allies and by Germany. The German commander von Lettow-Vorbeck engaged British forces for an extended period, undermining their efforts to send extra troops elsewhere in Europe and India. The war began when the British navy attacked Dar es Salaam and Tanga. The Germans retaliated by attacking

A company of German Askaris, from 1914 to 1918. It was usual for African to fight African on behalf of their colonial masters.

AFRICA, c. 1914

- area controlled by the Central Powers, 1914
- area controlled by the Allied powers, 1914
- neutral territory
- British advances
- French advances

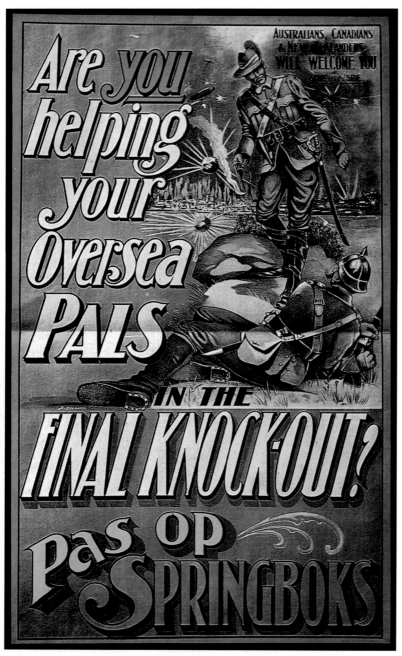

A British recruiting poster attempts to draw support from the white settler community in South Africa for its war in Europe.

the Uganda Railway around Mount Kilimanjaro. From Southern Africa, General Smuts advanced and attacked the Germans in the mountainous area near the Ruvu River. General Northey led the British attack from Northern Rhodesia and Nyasaland, while the Belgian army occupied Rwanda. In 1917 Pual von Lettow-Vorbeck invaded Mozambique and Northern Rhodesia.

With German defeat at the end of the war, France and Britain shared parts of Togo and Cameroon, Britain took Tanganyika, Belgium took Rwanda and Burundi, and South Africa took Southwest Africa. Darfur, which had allied itself with the Ottoman empire, was occupied and annexed to Sudan. Italian support for the Allies in Libya was compensated by the transfer of northern Kenya to its Somalia territory. All these states signed the League of Nations settlement, which "mandated" them to rule their conquered territories with guarantees of political independence and territorial integrity.

In East Africa, as many people died from famine and influenza as from the war itself. The experience of travel and bloodshed awakened the people to their oppression and led to agitation for political independence. Because they ate, slept, and fought together in the trenches, the war not only taught the Africans the strength of organized resistance, but exposed the weaknesses of the Europeans, especially the fact that they were not the masters of all knowledge. Briefly, the imperial powers strengthened their control over the colonies, but

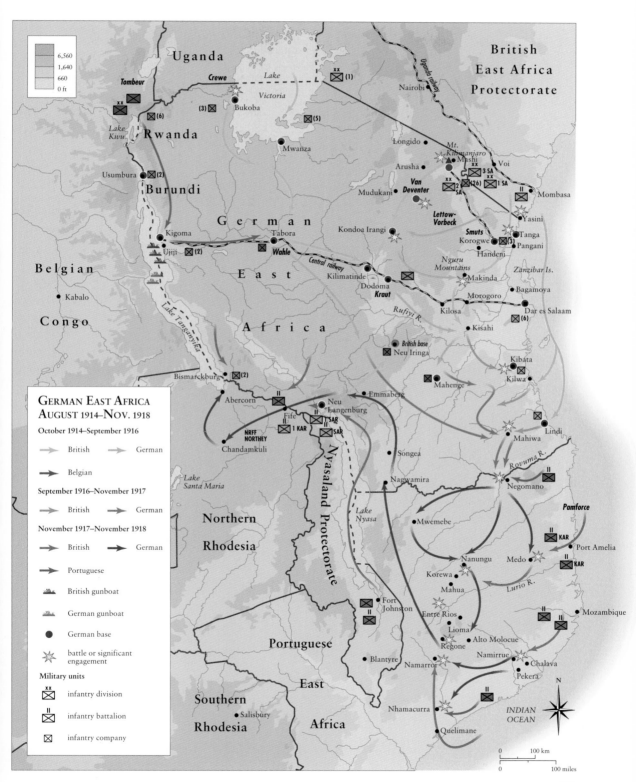

Uganda

Crewe

Lake Victoria

British East Africa Protectorate

Tombeur

⊠⊠ (1)

Nairobi

⊠ (6)

(3) ⊠ Bukoba

Lake Kivu

Rwanda

⊠ (5)

Mwanza

Longido

Mt. Kilimanjaro

Moshi

Voi

Usumbura ⊠ (2)

Arusha

Van Deventer

3 SA

Burundi

Mudukani

⊠⊠ (26)

2 SA

1 SA

Mombasa

Lettow-Vorbeck

Yasini

Kigoma

Tabora

Kondoa Irangi

Smuts

Tanga

Belgian

Ujiji ⊠ (2)

Wahle

Korogwe ⊠ (3)

Pangani

Handeni

Zanzibar Is.

G e r m a n

Central railway

Nguru Mountains

Kabalo

Kilimatinde

Makinda

E a s t

Dodoma

Bagamoya

Kraut

Morogoro

Congo

Rufiyi R.

Kilosa

Dar es Salaam ⊠ (6)

A f r i c a

Kisahi

British base

Neu Iringa ⊠

Kibata

Bismarckburg ⊠ (2)

Mahenge ⊠

Kilwa

Abercorn ⊠ II

Neu Langenburg

Emmaberg

Fife II

⊠ II

Lindi

NRFF NORTHEY

⊠ 1 KAR

SAR

Mahiwa

Chandamkuli

⊠ SAR

Songea

Rovuma R.

Negomano II

Lake Santa Maria

Nagwamira

Northern

Lake Nyasa

Mwemebe

Nanungu

Medo

Pamforce

II KAR

Port Amelia

Rhodesia

Korewa

Mahua

Lurio R.

II KAR

Fort Johnston II

Entre Rios

Mozambique

Portuguese

Lioma

Alto Molocue

II

II

Blantyre

Regone

Namirrue

Chalava

East

Namarror

Pekera

Southern

Salisbury

Africa

Nhamacurra

II

INDIAN OCEAN

Rhodesia

Quelimane

N

GERMAN EAST AFRICA
AUGUST 1914–NOV. 1918

October 1914–September 1916

→ British   → German

→ Belgian

September 1916–November 1917

→ British   → German

November 1917–November 1918

→ British   → German

→ Portuguese

🚢 British gunboat

🚢 German gunboat

● German base

✳ battle or significant engagement

Military units

⊠⊠ infantry division

II⊠ infantry battalion

⊠ infantry company

6,560

1,640

660

0 ft

---

0   100 km

0   100 miles

AFRICA IN WORLD WAR II

*British General
Sir Claude Auchinlake
inspects Free French
Senegalese troops, North
Africa, 1941.*

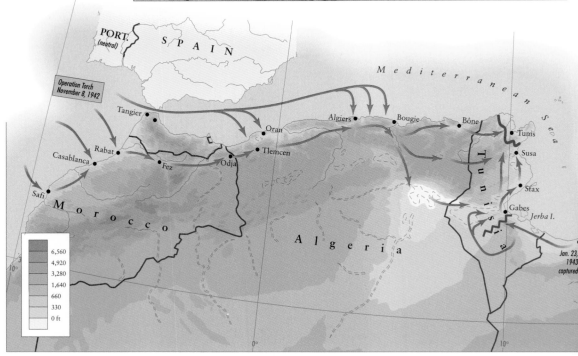

At the opening of the Second World War, British and French colonies in Africa were drawn into the conflict, but by then resistance to colonial rule had begun. This took the form of political organization by educated Africans, with some of the new leaders coming not from Africa itself but from the Caribbean, from India, and from America. In South Africa, J. L. Dube and Sol Plaatje were at the forefront; in Sierra Leone, J. Africanus Horton; and in Ghana, Casely Hayford.

In 1940, however, Germany conquered France, and some French colonies chose to support the new (Vichy) government. Both "Free France" and Britain began to recruit African soldiers.

In 1931, after the defeat of the Sanusi resistance, Italy had enjoyed total control of Libya, and in 1935, Mussolini conquered Ethiopia, occupying it until the British, with a large African force, liberated it in 1941.

Although African troops from South Africa were not allowed to hold firearms, they joined other Africans who came from East Africa (Uganda, Kenya, Tanzganyika, Somalia, Sudan, Nyasaland, and Rhodesia) and West Africa (Nigeria, Gold Coast, Sierra Leone, and Gambia) to fight alongside the Allied forces. The North African campaign began in 1941, with Africans again joining the British and Americans to fight against the Germans and Italians in Libya. Attacked on several fronts from Morocco, Algeria, and Egypt, and forced to retreat to Tunisia, the combined Italian-German army overwhelmed and was forced to surrender to Allied forces in 1943.

Considerable numbers of African soldiers fought in Burma, India, and Madagascar. The King's African Rifles contributed thirty battalions, with thousands of East Africans fighting in Asia against the Japanese. Eighty thousand fought in the French army in Europe. Many of these African soldiers read

African troops on the march, carrying with them Italian fascist emblems as souvenirs.

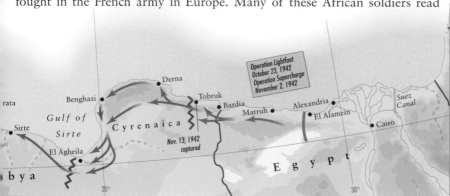

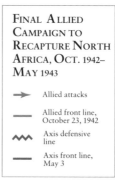

FINAL ALLIED CAMPAIGN TO RECAPTURE NORTH AFRICA, OCT. 1942–MAY 1943

→ Allied attacks

— Allied front line, October 23, 1942

⋀⋀ Axis defensive line

— Axis front line, May 3

widely and became well informed about world affairs, while at home colonial officials forced Africans to double their agricultural and mineral production in order to support the war effort. Shortages of essential goods as well as forced labor caused riots in different parts of the continent. Within settler communities, conflicts increased between whites and Africans, as many people moved from rural areas to the cities to seek employment. All these factors affected postwar political developments.

In East Africa, after the war there was a boom in the prices of agricultural products, but politically the war only increased people's resentment of the colonial administrators and their African representatives. This new political awareness resulted in an accelerated surge toward political independence. Blacks had fought alongside working-class whites and had come to regard them as equals. African soldiers, informed that this was a war for freedom, had fought and killed Europeans. The Africans' image of Europeans in their home countries changed, and there was increased journalistic interest as African servicemen abroad began writing home. Perhaps the most salutory experience of the war was the campaign against the Japanese, whose eventual defeat was greatly supported by African forces.

The British King's African Rifles accord the honors of war to the surrendering Italian garrison at Wolkefit near Gondar, Ethiopia, 1941.

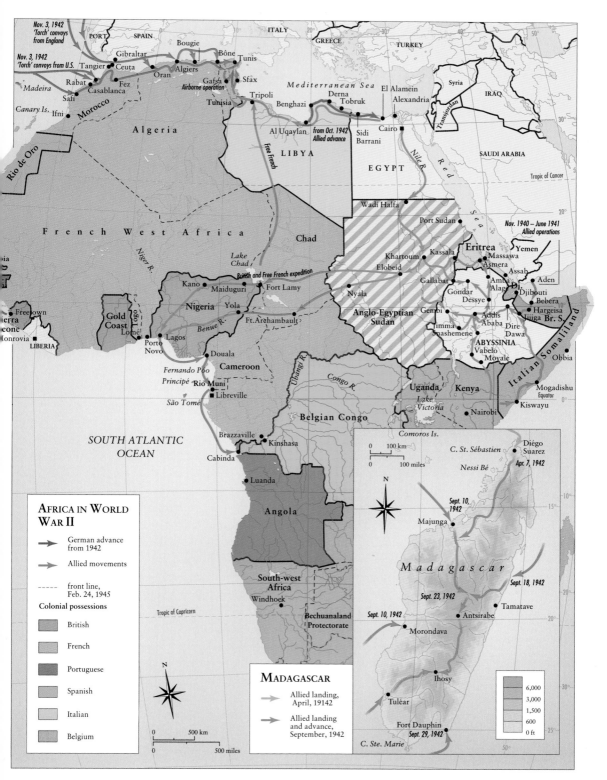

Nov. 3, 1942
'Torch' convoys
from England

Nov. 3, 1942
'Torch' convoys from U.S.

PORT. | SPAIN

Bougie

Gibraltar

Bône

Tunis

ITALY

GREECE

TURKEY

Tangier Ceuta

Algiers

Oran

Gafsa

Sfax

Madeira

Rabat

Fez

Casablanca

Safi

Airborne operation

Tripoli

Tunisia

Mediterranean Sea

Benghazi

Derna
Tobruk

El Alamein
Alexandria

Syria

IRAQ

Canary Is.

Ifni

Morocco

Al Uqaylan

from Oct. 1942
Allied advance

Sidi
Barrani

Cairo

Transjordan

SAUDI ARABIA

Rio de Oro

Algeria

LIBYA

Free French

EGYPT

Nile R.

Red Sea

Tropic of Cancer

Wadi Halfa

Nov. 1940 – June 1941
Allied operations

French West Africa

Chad

Lake
Chad

British and Free French expedition

Fort Lamy

Port Sudan

Khartoum

Elobeid

Kassala

Eritrea

Massawa
Asmera

Yemen

Assab

Niger R.

Kano

Maiduguri

Nyala

Gallabar

Amba
Alagi

Aden

Dj.

Djibouti

Bebera

ia

Freetown

rra

one

Monrovia

LIBERIA

Gold
Coast

Togo

Lomé

Nigeria

Lagos

Porto
Novo

Yola

Benue R.

Ft. Archambault

Anglo-Egyptian
Sudan

Gembi

Gondar

Dessye

Jimma

Snashemene

Gondar

Addis
Ababa

ABYSSINIA

Vabelo

Hargeisa

Jijiga Br. S.

Dire
Dawa

Moyalé

Italian Somaliland

Douala

Cameroon

Fernando Poo

Principé

Rio Muni

São Tomé

Libreville

Ubangi R.

Congo R.

Uganda

Lake
Victoria

Kenya

Nairobi

Mogadishu
Equator

Kiswayu

Obbia

SOUTH ATLANTIC
OCEAN

Brazzaville

Cabinda

Kinshasa

Belgian Congo

Comoros Is.

C. St. Sébastien

Nessi Bé

Diégo
Suarez

Apr. 7, 1942

0 | 100 km

0 | 100 miles

N

Luanda

Angola

Sept. 10,
1942

Majunga

AFRICA IN WORLD
WAR II

→ German advance
from 1942

→ Allied movements

----- front line,
Feb. 24, 1945

Colonial possessions

British

French

Portuguese

Spanish

Italian

Belgium

South-west
Africa

Windhoek

Tropic of Capricorn

N

Bechuanaland
Protectorate

MADAGASCAR

→ Allied landing,
April, 19142

→ Allied landing
and advance,
September, 1942

0 | 500 km

0 | 500 miles

Madagascar

Sept. 23, 1942

Sept. 10, 1942

Morondava

Tuléar

Ihosy

Fort Dauphin

Sept. 29, 1942

C. Ste. Marie

Sept. 18, 1942

Tamatave

Antsirabe

6,000

3,000

1,500

600

0 ft

133

LIBERATION WARS

French airborne troops, some of their men arriving at the checkpoint shortly after the demonstrations in Algiers. The war for Algerian independence would drag on from 1954 to 1962 with thousands losing their lives.

Algeria was taken over for French settlement as early as 1830. French colonists occupied the most fertile land, from which the indigenous owners were expelled, with disastrous effects on food production. The Algerians were suppressed and denied civil rights.

After 1945 a group of young nationalists, including Ahmed Ben Bella, formed the Front de Libération Nationale (FLN), which launched an armed struggle for freedom. Small in number and poorly armed, they fought ferocious battles against the French army. Alongside the military wing, a political wing was organized to spread propaganda and agitate for independence through demonstrations. The French fought the war with violent methods intended to eliminate the opposition, committing up to 70,000 troops to the struggle. The French settlers, faced with bloodshed and economic loss, also organized armed resistance to the government so as to persuade President de Gaulle to end the war. De Gaulle was obliged to negotiate with the FLN, and Algeria became independent in July 1962.

One of the longest and bloodiest liberation wars in Africa was that of the Mau-Mau in Kenya. When Kenya became a colony the whites settled in the Highlands, home of the Kikuyus, the country's largest ethnic group. The dispossessed Kikuyus were resettled in reserves, becoming squatters on plantations (*shambas*) owned by whites, who then coerced the colonial government into imposing taxes that would force the Africans to work for them. After the Second World War the Kikuyus became politicized by local leaders who encouraged them to form land and freedom armies. During the armed rebellion that started around 1952 they set up guerilla bases in the thick forests of the Aberdare Mountains and Mount Kenya. Led by Dedani Kimathi, the Mau-Mau struggle became bloody and violent as the British struggled to eliminate the rebels, whom they locked away in "protected villages." Part of the colonial army which fought against the freedom fighters was made up of Africans known as "home guards." Reacting to the bloodshed, British public opinion forced the colonial government to negotiate a political end to the rebellion and to the release of its foremost freedom fighter, Jomo Kenyatta. Since 1947 Kenyatta had been leader of the Kenya African Union, an organization established for unemployed or landless blacks, and since 1952 he had been in prison. Kenyatta was released in 1961, and Kenya achieved independence in 1963.

In central Africa, the settlers in Southern Rhodesia, who operated an oppressive system similar to that of the Boers in South Africa, resisted the call to give up their power and their land. Under an extremist white government led by Ian Smith, Rhodesia rebelled against Britain and declared its own independence

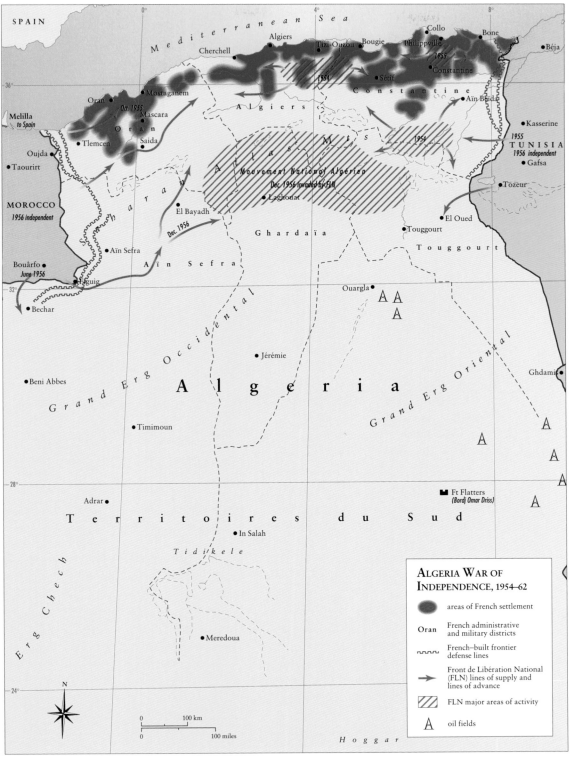

SPAIN

Mediterranean Sea

Collo
Bone
•Béja
Algiers
Tizi-Ouzou   Bougie   Philippville
Cherchell   *1955*
                                            Constantine
                                1954
•Mostaganem   *Sétif*
Oran •   C o n s t a n t i n e
     Oct. 1955   •Aïn Beïda
Melilla   Mascara   •Kasserine
to Spain   A l g i e r s
Tlemcen•   •Saida   *1955*
O r a n   TUNISIA
Oujda•   *1956 independent*
•Taourirt   *1954*   •Gafsa

MOROCCO   *A t l a s   M t s*   •Tozeur
1956 independent   *Mouvement National Algérien*
                        Dec. 1956 invaded by FLN
                        •Laghouat
        •El Bayadh   •El Oued
              Dec. 1956   G h a r d a ï a   •Touggourt
        •Aïn Sefra   T o u g g o u r t
Bouârfo•   A ï n   S e f r a
June 1956 Figuig
•Bechar   Ouargla• A A
                                          A
              •Jérémie
                                                      Ghdamis•
•Beni Abbes   A l g e r i a   *Grand Erg Oriental*
   Grand Erg Occidental
                                              A
        •Timimoun   A
                                          A
                                          A
Adrar•   ■ Ft Flatters   A
                          (Bordj Omar Driss)
  T e r r i t o i r e s   d u   S u d
  Tidikele   •In Salah

     N   •Meredoua

           0   100 km
           0   100 miles   *Hoggar*

ALGERIA WAR OF INDEPENDENCE, 1954–62

⬛ areas of French settlement

Oran — French administrative and military districts

〜〜〜 French–built frontier defense lines

➡ Front de Libération National (FLN) lines of supply and lines of advance

▨ FLN major areas of activity

A oil fields

Goodbye to Europe's hold on Africa. Children sit on the toppled statue of de Matos, founder of Nova Lisboa, the main town in Unita-held territory in Angola.

(UDI) in 1965. The government created a police state that denied the Africans any rights. The Africans nevertheless formed parties, the African National Congress of Southern Rhodesia (ANC), the Zimbabwe African People's Union (ZAPU), and the Zimbabwe African National Union (ZANU), a breakaway group from ZAPU. In 1966 armed resistance was started by guerillas trained in Zambia and Mozambique, where rebels were fighting the Portuguese. The war lasted until 1980, when the defeated settlers accepted elections based on one man, one vote.

After the partition the Portuguese continued to rule their colonies oppressively. While they practiced a policy of assimilation, like the French they denied Africans any rights or freedoms. In Guinea (Guinea-Bissau), Angola, and Mozambique, a very small percentage of the African population was assimi-lated and the vast majority remained *undigenas* (natives). In the three colonies, resistance groups were organized between 1956 and 1962: PAIGC in Portugese Guinea, MPLA in Angola, and FRELIMO in Mozambique. These soon turned to armed conflict, and wars of liberation began in Angola in 1961, in Guinea in 1963, and in Mozambique in 1964. They were extremely violent, and some local populations were decimated, but in the end Guinea won independence in 1974, Angola and Mozambique together with Cape Verde and São Tomé followed in 1975.

Namibians started campaigning for independence from South Africa rule after 1945. Two political organizations, the South West African Union (SWANU) formed in 1959, and the South West African People's Organization (SWAPO) in 1960, led the struggle. When the Organization for African Unity (OAU) and the United Nations pressured South Africa to relinquish its rule in Namibia, it proceeded to create bogus "homelands" and give various African peoples nominal independence. Namibia eventually gained full independence in 1990.

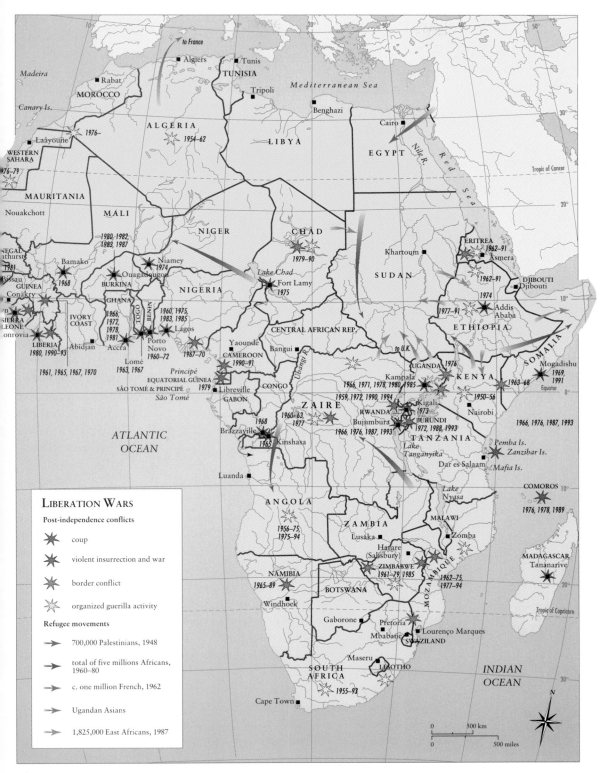

LIBERATION WARS

Post-independence conflicts

✴ coup

✴ violent insurrection and war

✴ border conflict

✴ organized guerilla activity

Refugee movements

➤ 700,000 Palestinians, 1948

➤ total of five millions Africans,
1960–80

➤ c. one million French, 1962

➤ Ugandan Asians

➤ 1,825,000 East Africans, 1987

INDEPENDENCE

The Second World War had an impact on Africa in a number of different ways. Africa's dependency on the production of raw materials for the European market was accelerated. Traditional societies disintegrated and the continent became increasingly urbanized. Ex-servicemen who came home from the war against racist German, Italian, and Japanese regimes strengthened the call by local politicians to free their countries from the colonialists' racism.

The nationalist struggles gathered momentum with the 1945 Manchester Pan-African conference, attended by people like Jomo Kenyatta (Kenya), George Padmore (West Indies), W. E. B. DuBois (United States), Kwame Nkrumah (Gold Coast/Ghana), and Namdi Azikiwe (Nigeria). Other leaders of early independence movements included Sekou Toure (French Guinea), Houphouet-Boigny (Ivory Coast), Julius Nyerere (Tanganyika/Tanzania) and Kenneth Kaunda (Northern Rhodesia/Zambia).

North of the Equator, Libya, led by King Idris al-Mahdi al-Sanusi, became a sovereignty in 1951. In Egypt, after a coup staged by the Free Officers in 1952, Gamal Abdel Nasser came to power. Morocco in 1955 and Tunisia in 1956 achieved their independence from France. Sudan became a republic in 1956. After a bloody struggle, which lasted almost seven years and cost a million lives, Algeria achieved independence in 1962. Somalia and Ethiopia, now including Eritrea, won freedom from Italy.

South of the Sahara, Ghana achieved independence from Britain in 1957, Nigeria in 1960, and The Gambia in 1965. In French West Africa, Guinea, led by Sekou Toure, declared its independence in 1958, followed by Senegal and Mali. These were in turn followed by Madagascar in 1960. Sierra Leone (Lion Mountain), a nation combining a colony settled by freed slaves or so-called Creoles and a protectorate of original inhabitants (Temme, Kisi, and Mende), gained independence in 1961.

In Congo, the most popular political parties were the nationally based Congolese National Movement (MNC) led by Patrice Lumumba (1925–1961) and the ethnically linked party, the Bakongo Alliance (ABAKO). The Belgians, after the Leopoldville rioting, decided to pull out in June 1960. They left the country disorganized and without middle-ranking administrators, and it broke up bloodily into independent mini-states such as Shaba (Katanga) led by Moise Tshombe, and Kasai province. Joseph Mobutu seized power in a coup three months later.

In East Africa, Kenyans fought the protracted Mau-Mau war from 1952 until 1956, and achieved independence from the British in 1963. Tanzania won independence in 1961, followed by Uganda in 1962. In central and southern Africa, the federated states of Southern Rhodesia, Northern Rhodesia, and Nyasaland were split, and in 1964 Northern Rhodesia (Zambia) and Nyasaland (Malawi) gained independence. Bechuanaland (Botswana) and Basutoland (Lesotho) became independent in 1966, followed by Swaziland in 1968.

Despite the "wind of change" sweeping through the continent, Portugal continued to assert control over its colonies. Nationalists initiated guerilla movements to drive the Portuguese from Angola, Cape Verde, Guinea (Guinea-Bissau) and

Mozambique. Within the former British colonies, Southern Rhodesia (Zimbabwe) also had to suffer a protracted guerilla war between whites and blacks before gaining independence in 1974. And Namibia had to fight a similar guerilla war against South Africa before it too could at last become a free nation.

African politics seemed to have changed forever in the 1960s, but the euphoria of independence turned out to be sadly short-lived.

ECONOMY AND TRADE

Since independence, the formation of trading blocks by African countries has been used to engender interstate unity, to promote economic growth, and to counter the ethnic divisions instituted by the colonial borders. Various blocks have been formed, some of which have disintegrated and some of which survive.

The East African Community (EAC) comprising Uganda, Kenya, Tanzania, and Zanzibar, formed in 1967 to develop joint services such as customs and excise, posts and telecommunications, railways, harbors, and airlines (East African Airways). Kenya, because of its strategic coastal ports and its colonial history, became the main beneficiary, and the Community broke up in 1977 during Idi Amin's reign in Uganda. Twenty years later, Yoweri Museveni of Uganda is attempting its revival, based on reworked agreements. As part of these new arrangements, citizens of Kenya, Uganda, and Tanzania may obtain an East African Passport allowing them to travel unrestricted throughout the region.

In 1975, sixteen former British and French colonial West African states, and Liberia, formed the Economic Community of West African States (ECOWAS) to develop a customs union and regional economic cooperation. Their main concerns were agriculture, energy, industry, telecommunications, and free trade. The community transcends the colonial borders, and has recently involved itself in solving political crises in the region, for example forming the 1990 multinational ECOMOG force to intervene in the Liberian civil war. Despite ECOWAS's commitment to the free movement of people across the borders of its member states, in 1983 Nigeria unilaterally expelled all of its foreign workers.

In 1980, the southern "frontline" states formed the Southern African Development Coordination Conference (SADCC) to promote economic cooperation and development. The chief purpose of this block was to combat the continuing sabotage of the economic, telecommunication, and transport facilities of its partner states. After 1993, the organization was renamed the Southern Africa Development Community (SADC), to mark the birth of the new free South Africa. Alongside the SADC is the Preferential Trade Area (PTA), which covers most eastern and central African states and aims to promote integrated interstate trade and industrial development. One of its main achievements is the creation of the UAPTA common currency, but since its formation this has met with difficulties caused by the economically more developed states like Kenya. Organizations like the SADC and ECOWAS also play a crucial role in negotiating and attracting foreign aid to the regions they represent. Presently there are plans to integrate the services offered by the SADC and the PTA.

Trading blocks formed by former French colonies have a higher survival rate. These include the L'Union Douanière et Économique de L'Ouest (UDEAL), which focuses on lowering custom duties and promoting economic development, L'Organization Commune Africaine et Mauricienne (OCAM), and La Communauté Économique de l'Afrique de L'Ouest (CEAO). The North African oil-exporting countries have together formed the Arab Bank for Economic Development (BADEA).

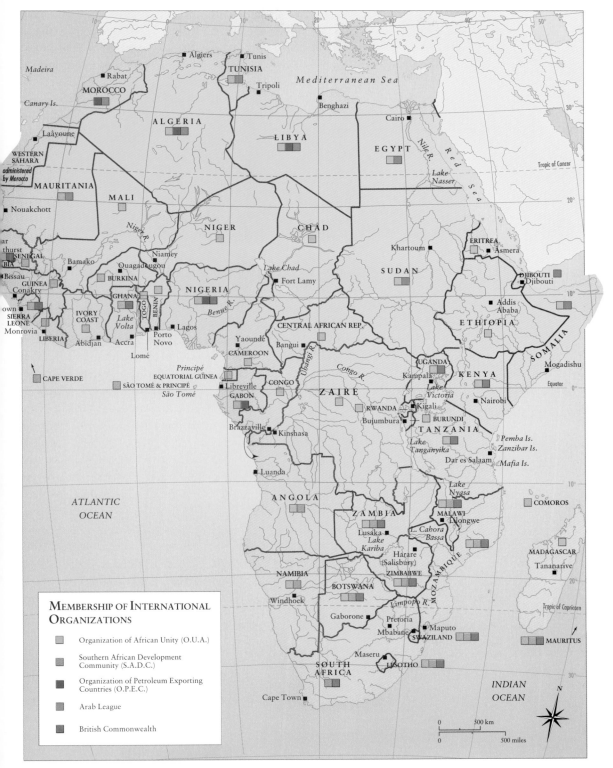

Madeira

■ Algiers   ■ Tunis

TUNISIA

■ Rabat   ■ Tripoli

MOROCCO

Canary Is.

■ Benghazi

Laâyoune

ALGERIA   LIBYA

■ Cairo

WESTERN
SAHARA
administered
by Morocco

EGYPT

Mediterranean Sea

Tropic of Cancer

Nile R.

*Lake
Nasser*

Red Sea

MAURITANIA

■ Nouakchott

MALI

Niger R.

NIGER   CHAD

■ Khartoum

ERITREA

■ Asmera

ar
thurst

SENEGAL

BIA

■ Bissau

GUINEA

■ Conakry

■ Bamako

NIGERIA

Niamey

■ Ouagadougou

BURKINA

GHANA

TOGO

BENIN

Benue R.

Fort Lamy

Lake Chad

SUDAN

DJIBOUTI

■ Djibouti

CENTRAL AFRICAN REP.

■ Addis
Ababa

ETHIOPIA

own

SIERRA
LEONE

■ Monrovia

LIBERIA

IVORY
COAST

*Lake
Volta*

■ Abidjan   ■ Accra

■ Lomé

■ Lagos

Porto
Novo

■ Yaoundé

CAMEROON

■ Bangui

Ubangi R.

UGANDA

■ Kampala

*Lake
Victoria*

KENYA

■ Nairobi

SOMALIA

■ Mogadishu

Equator

□ CAPE VERDE

Principé
EQUATORIAL GUINEA
SÃO TOMÉ & PRINCIPÉ
São Tomé

■ Libreville

CONGO

GABON

■ Brazzaville   ■ Kinshasa

Congo R.

ZAIRE

RWANDA

■ Kigali

BURUNDI

■ Bujumbura

*Lake
Tanganyika*

TANZANIA

■ Dar es Salaam

Pemba Is.
Zanzibar Is.
Mafia Is.

ATLANTIC
OCEAN

■ Luanda

ANGOLA

ZAMBIA

■ Lusaka

*Lake
Kariba*

L. *Cahora
Bassa*

*Lake
Nyasa*

MALAWI

■ Lilongwe

MOZAMBIQUE

□ COMOROS

MADAGASCAR

■ Tananarive

NAMIBIA

■ Windhoek

BOTSWANA

■ Gaborone

■ Harare
(Salisbury)

ZIMBABWE

Limpopo R.

■ Pretoria

■ Mbabane

■ Maputo

SWAZILAND

■ Maseru

SOUTH
AFRICA

LESOTHO

■ Cape Town

Tropic of Capricorn

MAURITUS

INDIAN
OCEAN

N

MEMBERSHIP OF INTERNATIONAL ORGANIZATIONS

☐ Organization of African Unity (O.U.A.)

☐ Southern African Development Community (S.A.D.C.)

☐ Organization of Petroleum Exporting Countries (O.P.E.C.)

☐ Arab League

☐ British Commonwealth

0   500 km

0   500 miles

SOUTH AFRICA, OLD AND NEW

The present shape of South Africa was formed in 1910 after the Anglo-Boer War of 1899–1902, which turned the two Afrikaaner territories Transvaal and Orange Free State into British colonies. In 1912 African activists formed the African Native National Congress, later named the African National Congress (ANC), to campaign for the advancement of black South Africans.

In 1920 the League of Nations gave South Africa a mandate to rule previously German-administered Southwest Africa, and there was provision for its High Commission states (Basutoland, Bechuanaland, and Swaziland) and Rhodesia to join a so-called South African Union. Despite South Africa's aggressive expansionist policies, Britain refused to have Swaziland incorporated into the Union, and in 1923 Rhodesia opted to become an independent state. Although Britain remained in control of all the High Commission territories, South Africa dictated the economics of these landlocked states.

South Africa's economic expansion had been generated by its vast mineral wealth, especially from the diamonds and gold discovered in the nineteenth century, but the outbreak of the Second World War forced the country to industrialize, increasing its dependence on urbanized black labor and its vulnerability to organized unrest. The apartheid (separateness) ideology developed during this period advocated the division of the country's whites and blacks, maintaining that there were distinctive differences between its various peoples and that each group should therefore live in its own "homeland" apart from the others. Miscegenation was outlawed, and Africans were forced to live on Native Reserves. After 1948 several measures including the Immorality Act, the Group Areas Act, the Separate Amenities Act, and the Bantu Education Act were introduced to reinforce apartheid. In 1959 the Promotion of Bantu Self-Government Bill gave "Bantustans" full political independence. On March 21, 1960, a peaceful

SOUTH AFRICA, OLD, 1926–94

- Republic of South Africa
- under South African mandate
- Bantustans
- South African attacks and intervention, 1975–88

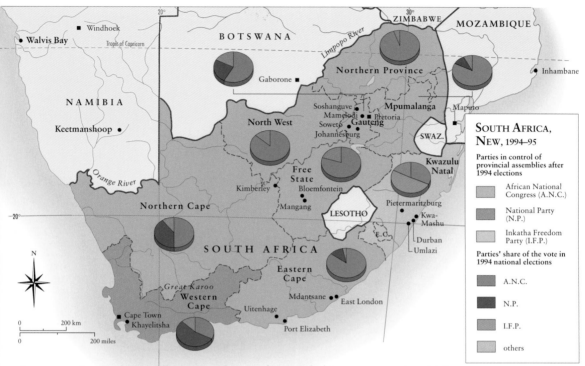

Walvis Bay · Windhoek ■
Tropic of Capricorn
NAMIBIA
Keetmanshoop ·
BOTSWANA
Gaborone ■
ZIMBABWE   MOZAMBIQUE
Limpopo River
· Inhambane
Northern Province
North West
Soshanguve
Mamelodi ■ Pretoria
Soweto · Gauteng
Johannesburg
Mpumalanga   Maputo ■
SWAZ.
Orange River
Free State
Kimberley ·   Bloemfontein ·
Mangang ·
LESOTHO
Northern Cape
Kwazulu Natal
Pietermaritzburg ·
Kwa-Mashu
E.C.   Durban
Umlazi
SOUTH AFRICA
Great Karoo
Western Cape
Eastern Cape
Mdantsane · East London
Uitenhage
Cape Town ■
Khayelitsha
Port Elizabeth

N

0   200 km
0   200 miles

SOUTH AFRICA, NEW, 1994–95

Parties in control of provincial assemblies after 1994 elections

African National Congress (A.N.C.)

National Party (N.P.)

Inkatha Freedom Party (I.F.P.)

Parties' share of the vote in 1994 national elections

A.N.C.

N.P.

I.F.P.

others

demonstration at Sharpeville against the pass laws ended in a massacre in which sixty-seven Africans were killed. Prime Minister Verwoerd's response was to hold a whites-only referendum, and in May 1961 to declare a South African Republic. Verwoerd's idea was that all nonwhites should be excluded from political life. ANC leader Nelson Mandela was tried and imprisoned in 1964.

Following a coup d'état in Portugal, in 1974 Angola and Mozambique declared their independence, and South Africa, backed by the United States, invaded Angola to install a UNITA government in place of the MPLA, supported by the Soviet Union and Cuba. These developments allowed SWAPO, which was fighting for the liberation of Namibia from within Angola, to start attacking the South African military stationed in Namibia. Meanwhile, FRELIMO, led by Samora Machel, had come to power, opening the border with Rhodesia and enabling guerillas to attack Ian Smith's regime from bases in Mozambique.

In 1976 South Africa experienced the Soweto uprisings, increasingly serious outbursts of black protest, and many whites began to realize that the country was heading for disaster. In 1989 free elections sponsored by the United Nations were held in Namibia, and its first independent government was instituted in 1990. Also in 1990, South Africa withdrew its forces from Namibia and Angola.

De Klerk's government legalized the ANC and released Nelson Mandela in February 1990. During the negotiations between the government, the ANC, the Pan African Congress (PAC), and the Inkatha Freedom (Zulu) Party, apartheid was dismantled and universal franchise elections were at last held in April 1994.

CHRONOLOGY

Many dates approximate

3-2 million BC Development of early hominids.

2,000,000-50,000 BC Early hominids in the savannah use simple tools.

50,000-15,000 BC Middle Stone Age. Use of fire and improved toolmaking. Early man spreads throughout continent.

8000 BC Emergence of *homo sapiens*. Earliest agriculture in North Africa.

5000 BC First agricultural and fishing settlements along the Nile River.

4000 BC Animal husbandry in the Nile Valley.

3500 BC Use of sailboats on the Nile River.

3200 BC King Narmer and King Menes unite Upper and Lower Egypt; start of Old Kingdom. Agriculture spreads southward to Central Africa.

2680 BC End of Egyptian Old Kingdom.

2650 BC Early Step Pyramid built at Saqqara. Spread of Sahara Desert begins.

2590 BC Great Pyramid of Cheops built.

2040 BC Egyptian Middle Kingdom begins. Renewal of pyramid building.

2060 BC Mentuhotep II establishes 11th dynasty at Herakleopolis.

1785 BC End of Egyptian Middle Kingdom.

1633 BC Egypt controlled by Hyksos, from Asia.

1570 BC Ahmose I drives Hyksos from Egypt.

1550 BC Reign of Kamose marks start of Egyptian New Kingdom. Egyptian power steadily extended to Nubia, Palestine, Lebanon, and Syria.

1500 BC Accession of Egyptian queen Hatshepsut.

1370 BC Akhenaten's campaign against polytheism.

1300 BC Egyptian-Hittite wars.

1166 BC Death of Rameses III.

1120 BC Phoenicians begin to control North Africa and Mediterranean; develop alphabetic script.

1085 BC Death of Rameses XI; end of Egyptian New Kingdom.

945 BC Civil war between Tanis and Thebes; decline of Egyptian power.

900 BC Kingdom of Cush (Nubia) established.

814 BC Phoenicians found Carthage.

730 BC Nubian king Pianky founds 25th dynasty to rule Egypt.

671 BC Assyrians conquer Egypt, introduce metalworking.

521 BC Persians build canal between Nile and Red Sea.

500 BC Ironworking spreads south of the Sahara. Growth of Nok culture in Nigeria.

334 BC Macedonian Alexander the Great invades Egypt, founds Alexandria.

304 BC Ptolemy I founds Macedonian dynasty in Egypt.

264-241 BC First Punic War between Carthage and Rome.

218-201 BC Second Punic War.

149-146 BC Third Punic War; Rome victorious, razes Carthage and founds province named Africa.

100 BC Romans introduce camels into the Sahara.

30 BC Death of Antony and Cleopatra; Egypt made a Roman province.

AD **44** Romans annex Mauretania (Morocco).

AD **50** Rise of Axum (Ethiopia).

AD **150** Berber and Mandingo control Sudan.

AD **189** Arrival of Christianity in North Africa.

AD **250** Axum controls Red Sea trade.

AD **325** Axum defeats Meroe kingdom (Cush).

AD **400** Indonesians start settling in Malagasy (Madagascar).

AD **428** Vandals invade northern Africa; collapse of Roman control.

500 Christianity spreading southward through Nubia.

533 Byzantine Christians overpower Vandals, install strong administration.

622 Mohammed's Hejira to Medina; year 1 in Islamic calendar.

632 Death of Mohammed, succeeded by Abu Bakr; start of Arab expansion.

639 Arabs invade Egypt and North Africa; collapse of Byzantine control; spread of Islam.

800 Rise of Ghana.

800   Arabs settle in

Madagascar.
969 Fatimids conquer Egypt and North Africa.
973 Fatimid caliph Al-Mu'izz establishes capital at Cairo, loses control of Maghrib (Tunisia, Algeria, Morocco).
1000 Ironworking in Zimbabwe.
1050 Height of Ghanaian empire. Bedouin raids on Egypt.
1056 Almoravid Muslims start conquest of North Africa.
1076 Almoravids start conquest of Ghana and Songhay. Almoravid capital established at Marrakesh.
1135 Almohad Muslims gain power in Morocco.
1150 Rise of Yoruba states (Nigeria).
1171 Saladin defeats Fatimids in Egypt; Ayyubid dynasty founded.
1200 Emergence of Hausa states (Nigeria).
1235 Defeat of Sosso (Ghana) by Malinke under Sundjata; growth of Mali empire . Al-Wahids found dynasty in Algeria.
1250 Ayyubids ousted by Turkish Mamelukes in Egypt. Marinid dynasty founded in Morocco.
1259 Death of Dunama Dibalemi (Kanem, Sudan). Bedouins spread into Maghrib.
1300 Capital of Kanem empire moved to Bornu. Rise of Benin. Walls of Great Zimbabwe constructed.
1324 Pilgrimage to Mecca of Malian emperor Mansa Musa.

1352 Arab historian Ibn Battutta's visit to Mali.
1360 Death of Mansa Sulayman (Mali).
1377 Death of Arab explorer and geographer Ibn Battuta.
1415 Portuguese capture Ceuta; start of Portugal's empire.
1425 Growth of Karanga (Shona) Mwanamutapa empire under Mutota.
1434 Portuguese extend south of Cape Bojador.
1450 Height of empire of Songhay. Matope succeeds Mutota.
1464 Accession of Sonni Ali in Songhay; start of opposition to Mali.
1471 Portuguese control Almina (Gold Coast).
1468 Sonni Ali captures Timbuktu.
1480 Death of Matope. empire splits into Mwanamutapa and Rozwi (south of the Zambezi). Wattasid dynasty established in Morocco.
1483 French found settlement in Senegal.
1487 Portuguese trading post established in Benin.
1492 Spanish start settling North African coast.
1505 Portuguese trading posts established in Mozambique and along eastern coast. Growth of transatlantic slave trade.
1546 Mali empire overthrown by Songhay.
1571 Portuguese found settlement in Angola, build forts along the Zambezi.

1578 Moroccans defeat Portuguese at battle of al-Ksa Kebir.
1580 Accession of Idris Alooma; height of Bornu-Kanem empire.
1591 Moroccans and Spanish defeat Songhay at battle of Tondibi.
1592 Portuguese build Fort Jesus (Mombasa).
1600 Rise of Oyo empire.
1613 Portuguese found colonies on Madagascar.
1628 Portuguese defeat Mwanamutapa empire.
1652 Dutch establish Cape Colony.
1659 French trading posts in Senegal.
1662 Portuguese victorious at battle of Ambuila; control Congo.
1700 Rise of Ashanti empire (Gold Coast/Ghana).
1725 Islamic jihads begin in Guinea.
1730 Revival of Bornu-Kanem.
1779 First Xhosa war against Dutch in southern Africa.
1787 Rise of the Oyo empire. Accession of Andrianampoinimerina in Madagascar; spread of European influence.
1798 French under Napoleon invade Egypt; Mamelukes defeated at battle of Imbaba.
1802 Death of Usman dan Fodio, Fulani Islamic warrior.
1804 Fulanis defeat Hausa.
1806 Cape Colony captured by British.

1811 Mohammed Ali rules Egypt. Fourth Xhosa war against British.

1817–1836 Busaidi-Mazrui struggle for control of east coast trade.

1818 Shaka becomes king of Zulus.

1821 Egyptian Muhammad Ali invades Sudan.

1822 Liberia founded for freed slaves.

1830 Muhammad Ali establishes capital of Sudan at Khartoum. French invade Algeria. Decline of the Oyo empire. European explorations of the Niger River area.

1833 Abolition of slavery throughout British empire.

1834 Sixth Xhosa war; British control all Xhosa land. Boers' Great Trek from Cape begins.

1836–1838 Boer-Ndebele battles.

1839 Boers found Natal.

1848 Boers found Orange Free State and Transvaal.

1853-1871 Livingstone's explorations of Central Africa.

1860 French expansion from Senegal.

1869 Completion by French engineers of Suez Canal (Egypt).

1874 British defeat Ashanti, establish Gold Coast colony. De Brazza's and Stanley's expeditions to Congo.

1875 British acquire Suez Canal. Zimba raids on east coast towns; Mombasa destroyed.

1879 Zulus defeat British at battle of Isandlwana. British defeat Zulus at battle of Ulundi.

1881 French invade Tunisia.

1882 British occupy Egypt; Mahdist revolt in Sudan. French ratify De Brazza's "treaties" in Central Africa.

1884 The Berlin Conference on the partition of Africa. Germans gain South West Africa (Namibia), Cameroons, Togoland, and Tanganyika (German East Africa). Belgian King Leopold gains Congo (Zaire). French control Senegal, Ivory Coast, French Guinea, Dahomey, Gabon. British control Gold Coast, Nigeria, Sierra Leone, Gambia, and Uganda. Portuguese control Angola, Mozambique, and Guinea-Bissau.

1886 Partition of East Africa between British and Germans. Discovery of gold in Transvaal; foundation of Johannesburg.

1889 Cecil Rhodes' British South Africa Company gains control of eastern Central Africa. French control Djibouti.

1895 Jameson's raid into Transvaal.

1896 Ethiopians overcome Italians at the battle of Adowa.

1898 Mahdists defeated in Sudan by British and Egyptians at the battle of Omdurman. German South Cameroons Company established. Maji-Maji rebellion in Tanganyika.

1899 Boers declare war on British in South Africa. Siege of Mafeking.

1900 British establish protectorate in Nigeria. French defeat Rabih ibn Fadl Allah's jihad in Sudan. First concentration camp established in Boer war.

1902 Boer resistance crushed.

1904 Hehero and Hottentot rebellions against Germans.

1908 Belgian state administers Congo. Italians occupy Libya, Eritrea, and Somalia.

1910 British Union of South Africa established.

1912 Birth of ANC in South Africa.

1914–1918 World War I. British claim Egypt as a protectorate. British and French seize German colonies of Kenya, Tanganyika, Togo, and Cameroon. South Africa takes over German South West Africa (Namibia).

1919 Nationalist rebellion in Egypt.

1921 Spanish defeated by Moroccans at battle of Anual.

1931 Italians defeat Sanusiyya, strengthen control of Libya.

1934 South Africa becomes independent.

1935 Italians invade Ethiopia.

1936 British fortify Suez Canal.

1940 World War II. Italians invade Egypt.

1941 British take Tobruk, defeat Italians in Somalia, Eritrea, Ethiopia. Germans land in Tripoli; Rommel pushed back to Al Agheila.

1942 Rommel counter-attacks, advances toward Egypt. British victorious at El Alamein. US landings on North African coast.

1943 Allies take Tunis. Axis forces driven from North Africa.

1945 Pan-African conference in Manchester, England.

1948 Nationalist rebellion in Madagascar crushed by French. National Party introduces racist apartheid policy in South Africa.

1951 Libya declares sovereignty under Idris al-Mahdi.

1952 Revolution in Egypt; Gamal Abdel-Nasser becomes president. Eritrea federated with Ethiopia. Start of Mau-Mau rebellion against British in Kenya.

1954 Suez Canal crisis; British withdrawal. Ahmed Ben Bella leads FLN in war of independence in Algeria.

1955–1972 Civil war in Sudan.

1956 Tunisia wins independence from France.

1957 Ghana (formerly Gold Coast) wins independence from Britain; Kwame Nkrumah president.

1958 Guinea wins independence from France.

1960 Mauretania, Benin (Dahomey), Niger, Togo, Burkina (Upper Volta), Senegal, French Cameroon, Gabon, Ivory Coast, Central African Republic (CAR), Mali, Chad, and Madagascar win independence from France. Nigeria and Somalia win independence from Britain. Congo (Zaire) wins independence from Belgium; Katanga (Shaba) secedes; UN intervention in ensuing war.

Sharpeville massacre in South Africa; South Africa leaves British Commonwealth.

1961 Tanzania formed (a union of Tanganyika and Zanzibar) and with Sierra Leone wins independence from Britain. Eritreans begin armed struggle for independence from Ethiopia. Independence movements mobilize in Southern Rhodesia. Liberation war begins in Angola.

1962 Ceasefire in Algeria; declared independent republic under Ben Bella. Uganda gains independence from Britain. Rwanda and Burundi gain independence from Belgium; Hutu persecution of Tutsi begins; Tutsis exiled.

1963 Kenya wins independence from Britain; Jomo Kenyatta prime minister. Liberation war begins in Guinea-Bissau. Organization for African Unity (OAU) formed.

1964 Zambia (Northern Rhodesia) under Kenneth Kaunda and Malawi (Nyasaland) win independence from Britain. FRELIMO begins guerilla war of liberation in Mozambique. Ethiopia-Somalia war over Ogaden region. In South Africa ANC leader Nelson Mandela jailed.

1965 Coup in Central African Republic led by Jean-Bédel Bokassa; builds personal empire. Gambia wins independence from Britain. Ian Smith declares State of Emergency in

Southern Rhodesia and UDI from Britain; guerilla war escalates, trade sanctions imposed. Military junta ousts Ben Bella in Algeria.

1966 Military coup in Burundi. Botswana (Bechuanaland) and Lesotho (Basutoland) gain independence from South Africa. SWAPO starts armed struggle against South Africans in Namibia. Libyan insurgency into Chad.

1966–1970 Military coup in Nigeria leads to bloody civil war and famine.

1969 Coup in Libya led by Colonel Gaddafi; revolutionary anti-Western regime installed.

1970 Mobutu Sese Seko elected president of Zaire. Death of Nasser; succeeded by Anwar Sadat.

1971 Completion by Russian engineers of Aswan High Dam (Egypt); end of Soviet influence.

1972 Ethnic strife and anarchy in Uganda under Idi Amin; expulsion of Asians. Massacre of Hutus by Tutsi in Burundi. Peace agreement in Mauretania.

1975 Angola wins independence from Portugal; civil war ensues between MPLA and UNITA; South Africa intervenes. Mozambique wins independence from Portugal; FRELIMO leader Samora Machel becomes president; supports freedom fighters in Zimbabwe (Rhodesia). Civil war continues between FRELIMO and REN-AMO.

1976 Soweto uprisings in South Africa.

1977 Hostilities between Libya and Egypt.

1978 Somali attacks on Ethiopia repelled. Martial law in Congo.

1979–1982 Christian-Muslim civil war in Chad.

1979 Coup in Ghana led by Flight-Lieutenant Jerry Rawlings.

1980 New constitution and independence for Zimbabwe (Southern Rhodesia); Robert Mugabe elected prime minister. Coup in Liberia led by Samuel Doe.

1981 Egyptian President Sadat assassinated; Muslim extremism spreads. Two Libyan jets shot down by US.

1983 Muslim fundamentalist rebellion in southern Sudan; severe drought. Civil war in Cameroon.

1984 Morocco and Libya sign cooperation treaty; start of Maghrib Union; bread riots in Tunisia.

1985 Foreigners expelled from Libya; diplomatic links severed.

1986 US air raid to kill Gaddafi unsuccessful. P. W. Botha declares state of emergency in South Africa. President Museveni comes to power in Uganda; ethnic conflict subsides.

1987 Libyans expelled from Chad. Tribal unrest in Zimbabwe; Mugabe re-elected president.

1988 Further massacre of Hutus in Burundi.

1989 Arab Maghrib Union (AMU) formed (Morocco, Algeria, Tunisia, Libya, Mauretania). Libya-Chad peace agreement. F. W. De Klerk elected, steers South Africa toward reform.

1990 Civil war in Liberia; Doe ousted. Namibia wins independence. Tutsi invasion of Rwanda. ANC unbanned in South Africa. South Africa withdraws from Angola and Namibia. Unrest grows in Zaire.

1991 Islamic party wins election in Algeria but is denied power by a military coup; campaign of violence follows. Eritrea secedes from Ethiopia. Tribal conflict and famine in Somalia. Uprising in Djibouti. Muslim fundamentalist regime in Sudan. Liberian incursions into Sierra Leone. UN-supervised peace in Angola; MPLA win elections.

1992 Peace agreement in Mozambique. UN peacekeeping mission to Somalia proves abortive. Coup in Sierra Leone led by Captain Strasser.

1993 UNITA resumes war in Angola. Military coup in Burundi. Government collapses in Zaire. Constitutional transition in South Africa.

1994 Multiracial, multiparty constitution in South Africa; Nelson Mandela elected President. US troops withdrawn from Somalia.

1996 Rwandan refugee crisis.

1997 End of Mobutu's regime in Zaire. Muslim fanatics massacre tourists in Luxor, Egypt. Europeans seek to intervene in worsening Algerian emergency.

SELECT BIBLIOGRAPHY

The author readily acknowledges the work of many scholars and publications that have been consulted in the preparation of this atlas. Following is a selected bibliography of works recommended for further reading on the topics covered in this atlas.

Ade Ajayi, J. F., and Crowder, Michael, *Historical Atlas of Africa*, London: Longman Group Ltd, 1985

Afigbo, A .E., et al., *The Making of Modern Africa, Volume 2,* London: Longman Group Ltd., 1986

Afrigbo, A. F., et al., *The Making of Modern Africa, Volume 1*, London: Longham, 1986

Amin, Samir, *The Maghreb in the Modern World: Algeria, Tunisia, Morocco,* London: Penguin Books Ltd., 1970

Ayittey, George, N. B., *Africa Betrayed*, New York: St. Martin's Press Inc, 1993

Buah, F. H., *West Africa and Europe,* London: Macmillan Education Ltd., 1981

Chaliand, Gerard, and Rageau, Jean-Pierre, *The Penguin Atlas of Diasporas*, London: Penguin Books Ltd., 1995

Davidson, Basil, et al., *The Growth of African Civilisation: East and Central Africa to the Late Nineteenth Century,* London: Longman Group UK Ltd., 1972

Davidson, Basil, *Africa in Modern History: The Search for a New Society,* London: Penguin Books, 1987
Modern Africa: A Social and Political History, London: Longman Group UK Ltd., 1989
Discovering Africa's Past, London: Longman Group Ltd., 1984
The Story of Africa, London: Mitchell

Beazley Publishers, 1984
Africa in History: Themes and Outlines, London: Phoenix, 1991
The African Slave Trade, London: Back Bay Books, 1980

Fage, J. D., and Arnold, Edward, *An Atlas of African History*, London: Edward Arnold Publisher Ltd.

Fage, J. D., *A History of West Africa,* Cambridge University Press, 1972

Fage, J. D., *A History of Africa*, London: Unwin Hyman Ltd., 1988

Griffiths, Ieuan, L. L., *The African Inheritance,* London: Routledge, 1995

Grinkers, Richard Roy, and Steiner, B. Christopher, *Perspective on Africa: A Reader in Culture, History and Representation*, Oxford: Blackwell Publishers, 1997

James, Lawrence, *The Rise and Fall of the British Empire*, London: Little, Brown and Company (UK), 1994

Lovejoy, Paul, E., *Transformations in Slavery: A History of Slavery in Africa,* Cambridge: Cambridge University Press, 1983

Mamdani, Mahmood, *Citizen and Subject: Contemporary Africa and the Legacy of Late Colonialism,* Princeton: Princeton University Press, 1996

Manley, Bill, *The Penguin Historical Atlas of Ancient Egypt,* London: Penguin Books Ltd., 1996

Martin, M., and O'Meara, Partick, ed., *Africa,* Indianapolis: Indiana University Press, 1995

McEvedy, Colin, *The Penguin Atlas of African History,* London:

Penguin Books Ltd., 1995

McEvedy, Colin, and Jones, Richard, *Atlas of World Population History*, London: Penguin Books Ltd., 1978

Mokhtar, G., ed., *General History of Africa II: Ancient Civilisations of Africa*, London: Heinemann, 1981

Moore, R. I., ed., *The Hamlyn Historical Atlas,* London: Hamlyn Publishers, 1981

Ogot, B. A., Zamani: *A Survey of East African History*, Nairobi: East African Publishing House, 1973

Oliver, Roland, and Atmore, Antony, *Africa Since 1800*, Cambridge: Cambridge University Press, 1977

Omer-Cooper D., et al., *The Growth of African Civilisation: The Making of Modern Africa, Volume I*, London: Longman Group Ltd., 1972

Pakenham, Thomas, *The Scramble for Africa,* London: ABACUS, 1991

Rotberg, Robert I., ed., *Africa and Its Explorers: Motives, Methods, and Impact*, Cambridge, Massachusetts: Harvard University Press, 1973

Shepherd, W. R., *Historical Atlas*, New York: Barnes & Noble, Inc., 1964

Shillington, Kevin, *History of Africa*, London: Macmillan Education Ltd., 1995

Stone, Norman, ed., *The Times Atlas of World History, Third Edition,* London: Times Books Limited

Walvin, James, *Black Ivory: A History of British Slavery*, London: Rex Collins Publisher, 1992

Webster, J. B., et al., *The Revolutionary Years: West Africa Since 1800*, London: Longman Group Ltd., 1980

Wesseling, H. L., *Divide and Rule: The Partition of Africa, 1880-1914,* Westport: Praeger Publishers, 1996

Wilson, S. H., *African Decolonisation*, London: Edward Arnold, 1994

Wilson, Derek, A., *A Student's Atlas of African History*, London: University of London Press Ltd., 1973

Index

ACKNOWLEDGMENTS

Pictures are reproduced by permission of, or have been provided by the following:

Bettmann/UPI: p. 110.
British Museum: pp. 30, 34.
e.t. archive: pp. 10, 38, 41, 49, 64, 66, 70, 80, 91, 96, 98, 100, 106, 108, 110, 114, 127.
Getty: pp. 82, 84, 86, 88, 93, 104, 118, 120, 121, 126, 134, 136.
Imperial War Museum: pp. 130, 131, 132.
The Image Bank: pp. 13, 16, 24, 27, 32, 60, 111.
Peter Newark's Historical Pictures: pp. 102, 125, 127.
Magnum: p. 18.
National Army Museum—London: p. 122.
Werner Forman Archive: pp. 44, 46, 48, 50, 52, 54, 68, 72, 78.
and Private Sources

Illustrations: Peter A. B. Smith and M. A. Swanston.

Design: Malcolm Swanston.

Typesetting: Shirley Ellis, Marion M. Storz.

Cartography: Peter Gamble, Elsa Gibert, Peter A. B. Smith, Malcolm Swanston, Isabelle Verpaux, Jonathan Young.

Production: Marion M. Storz.